Ready, Set, Sell!

HOW TO GET FROM ZERO TO SALES HERO IN 90 DAYS

Ready, Set, Sell!

HOW TO GET FROM ZERO TO SALES HERO IN 90 DAYS

BY DON MASTRANGELO

Power Plan Press

Prescott, Arizona

Published by Power Plan Press
P.O. Box 1788
Prescott, Arizona 86302
(800) 688-0999

ISBN 0-9768280-0-6
Library of Congress Control Number: 2005906767

Project management and editing by Via Press, LLC www.via-press.com
Design by Sample Design www.sampledesign.com
Indexing by Margaret Hentz

Printed in the United States of America

1 2 3 4 5 6 7 8 9 10

This book is dedicated to the many hundreds of individuals who, over the years, have encouraged and inspired me to share this information with the worldwide sales community.

My sincere appreciation goes to Rachel, Mary, and Nicholas for allowing me to prioritize the time to write this book.

Thanks to Louis, Anthony, and many others for the countless hours of support.

Thank you Jacqui for starting me out on the right foot and believing in me!

TABLE OF CONTENTS

PREFACE

Welcome! If you are reading this book, you are probably considering a career in sales or are a salesperson just getting started. You might be one of the thousands who has been "downsized" and are starting over in an entirely new career. Maybe you have been out of the work force for a while raising your children and are thinking about going back to work through a full- or part-time sales job. You could be a sales manager or business owner hoping that this book will offer you and your sales team a straightforward, clear, and concise plan to quickly become successful at your company.

It doesn't matter what you are selling. You can be selling to small businesses, individuals, families, or large corporations. You might be selling enterprise software solutions or encyclopedias, advertising or wireless phones, a network marketing opportunity, insurance, or anything in between. It doesn't matter because the process I will teach you is the same regardless of the product or service you are offering.

I have invested my entire career learning, following, testing, and proving how to get from zero to sales hero in 90 days. The principles and procedures outlined in this "Ready, Set, SELL! System" are timeless. I have made it my life's ambition to package and present this information so that even the newest salesperson can quickly learn what it takes to be successful, including all the information needed to create personalized objectives and a specific 90-day action plan. In addition, it is just as simple to use this process to build or rebuild a sales team to sell your product or service! I have personally helped hundreds of individuals of all ages and backgrounds with all types of personalities break through their fears and concerns to become extremely successful in sales. It has been very rewarding for me to see their eyes open and for these "new" salespeople to realize that success is not a mystery, and that any person who really wants to be successful in sales can be — it's simply a matter of choice. By following the steps outlined here with a positive attitude and enthusiasm YOU can become your organization's sales HERO in the next 90 days! Everything you need to know is at your disposal in this brief but powerful book.

Read this book tonight and begin your journey to success tomorrow!

Like any worthwhile book on selling, *Ready, Set, SELL!* fills a specific niche. As you will see, it is an indisputable, proven selling process. However, you will need the motivation and personal commitment to follow it. You may find that although the process is simple, you are having a hard time getting yourself to consistently do what you need to do, when you need to do it. There are excellent books and other resources available that can help you overcome your challenges and find your motivation. (*Unlimited Power* and *Awaken the Giant Within* by Anthony Robbins are terrific examples. I still have an original, autographed hardcover copy of *Unlimited Power* on my desk. It was one of the first personal development books I read and it made a huge impact on my success.) In addition, once you commit to the RSS System and start your 90-day journey to success, you will need to continue to hone your selling skills and devote yourself to an ongoing personal development program. Reading *at least* ten pages per day written by Brian Tracy, Zig Ziglar, Tom Hopkins, Stephen Covey, Anthony Robbins, Kenneth Blanchard and Spencer Johnson, Jeffrey Gitomer, or some of the other masters of selling and personal development will help you to build a truly successful sales career. For a list of these resources, visit the RSS System website at *www.donmastrangelo.com.*

As a profession, selling offers one of the best lifestyles available today. And — if you are still wondering — YES! YOU CAN DO IT! I don't care what you have or haven't done before today. Selling is the only profession that will accept you at any level, regardless of age, past experience, or education, while providing you with the opportunity to earn an unlimited income. Unfortunately, many new salespeople fail or quit within the first few months. The most common story is that after a short training program almost entirely focused on the product or service to be sold, the salesperson is sent out to the field with instructions to "sell, sell, sell!"

For example, Cindy takes a position with ABC Wireless and is very excited about the opportunity to earn a sizeable commission for each cellular phone plan she sells. While in training she has learned all about the different phones and rate plans she has to offer, as well as everything she could learn about her competitors and how to position her products against theirs. Cindy believes that she is ready to get out there and start selling!

Day One: Cindy makes a handful of prospecting calls and gets mostly "No's." On day two she gets similar results. By the end of the first week she has at best a few "warm" prospects. Cindy starts wondering if she made a mistake. Maybe the opportunity is not as good as she was led to believe. The market seems to be saturated. Or maybe she is just not cut out for this — after all, she has no experience and she's obviously doing something wrong because nobody wants to buy from her. She hears comments from some of the other sales reps that make her believe that they are also discouraged. Over the next few weeks she keeps trying, but her confidence is waning and she does less and less prospecting. By the end of the month she has mentally given up. She stays on until her draw runs out or she finds another job.

Success Is Simple – But Not Easy!

Cindy just did not know what to do to be successful. What she needed — in addition to a better understanding of what to expect — was a precise action plan that would produce a predictable and measurable outcome in a short period of time. Cindy would have been able to follow the plan and compare her actual results to the predicted results of the plan. If she could have seen that her actions were creating the desired results, she would have been more likely to maintain her confidence and keep her activity level high enough to create the necessary momentum. She failed because she simply did not have a clear picture of exactly what to do and what results to expect. Inevitably, Cindy became discouraged and gave up.

For years I have taught the RSS System through seminars across the country. In many cases, participants are new at sales. I have made it a habit to ask these individuals why they chose sales as a profession. The typical responses include the ability to earn an unlimited income, the freedom to enjoy a relatively flexible schedule once success has been achieved, and the desire to have more control over their overall destiny. Often I'll hear comments like, "People always tell me I'd be good at sales because of my personality."

Then I'll ask what, if anything, scares or concerns them about going into sales. The participants usually answer:

I don't want to make someone buy something they don't need or want.

Prospecting scares me to death!

Good salespeople are fast talkers – but I'm not like that.

I hate being rejected.

At this point I'll ask for examples of the "worst salesperson you have ever met." These stories usually go like this:

A salesperson came into our office and was so obnoxious.

You wouldn't believe what this one guy did.

…and she just kept talking even though I told her I was late for another appointment.

He never listened to anything I said.

He took the order and we never saw him again.

She told me everything there was to know about her product even though I told her we were not interested.

Pushy…Rude…Wouldn't take no for an answer.

Next, I'll ask for examples of experiences with "great" salespeople whom they would gladly do business with again:

She listened to what I had to say and was sincerely interested in helping me…

He knew his product very well and showed me how it would save us money.

The Stereotypical Salesperson

He asked a lot of questions and only sold us what we needed.

She was always available when we needed help.

You get the idea.

The most common concerns about becoming a salesperson are always connected to the stereotypical "worst" salesperson. Many assume that those are the ones who make the most money when in fact that is rarely the case!

To overcome these fears and concerns, you need to learn to operate like the "great" salespeople! The difference in the approach is that a great salesperson embraces a natural and effective process that I refer to as "relationship selling." Relationship selling focuses on the needs of the prospect rather than the needs of the salesperson. The salesperson will get what he wants as a by-product of helping enough prospects get or achieve what they need – and only what they need. Great salespeople don't "make" people buy. Rather, they do whatever it takes to "find" prospects who have a need for their product or service.

It is essential to understand that not everyone perceives an immediate need for your product or service. Your role is to talk to everyone (who fits your profile), determine if the need is there, and sell to fill the need. Every completed prospecting call is a success regardless of the outcome. Relationship selling allows you to initiate and develop long-term, mutually beneficial relationships with your customers. Some will buy sooner and some later. You will be able to gain referrals and repeat business in a way that the "fast-talking" salesperson never will. The process of relationship selling is covered in detail later in this book.

You will create the foundation for your own success or failure through your first few weeks of sales activity, and you will either succeed or fail within 90 days. Cindy never had a chance. You, however, have the RSS System, and you will have a thorough understanding of how to invest a tremendous amount of energy into a short period of time to create the kind of momentum most never achieve. The first 90 days will be intense and possibly exhausting, but also exhilarating and rewarding. Most importantly, what you accomplish in only three short months can carry you through indefinitely. Once you have paid the price, you will never have to work at the same pace again unless you start with a new company, industry, or venture. Even then, it's never as hard as the first time!

I challenge you to read this book to completion today, set your personal objectives and create your action plan tonight, and start your 90-day journey to success tomorrow!

INTRODUCTION

I really can't remember a time in which I wasn't selling SOMETHING. When I was in the fifth grade, my brother and I loved a snack called "Hot-Picks." They were hot cinnamon toothpicks sold by the dozen in a wax paper package. When our convenience store stopped selling them, we decided to make our own. We went to the drug store, bought a supply of toothpicks, and somehow convinced the pharmacist to sell us cassia oil — basically pure cinnamon extract.

Once home, we simply poured some cassia oil into a bowl, dropped in a pile of toothpicks, and let them soak for a few hours. Then we placed them on a paper towel to dry. The whole process took a little trial and error, but it was simple enough.

I stuck one in my mouth and WOW!, those things were HOT — I mean REALLY hot! That cassia oil could burn the heck out of you if you got too much on your skin. Once we figured out how to handle them without getting burned, we and our friends liked them a lot. It didn't take long for word to get around, and we started selling our own version of hot-Picks at school for 25 cents a bag. This venture lasted exactly one day. Apparently, many of our customers ended up burning their lips, noses, and eyes. Once enough of them were in the nurse's office, word got to the principal, who tracked down the source of this plague. My brother and I were summoned to the office for a very stern lecture.

That same year, I started my next venture. One day I bought a five pack of "Bubble-Yum" bubble gum for 25 cents on the way to school. At recess, a kid who saw me chewing and blowing bubbles offered to buy a piece for 25 cents, and I gladly obliged! Soon, some other kids came over. Since the standard was set at 25 cents a piece, I quickly sold the remaining three pieces. I started by investing a quarter in a pack of gum and suddenly I had a dollar and one piece of gum for myself.

The next morning I bought four more packs of gum on the way to school and sold all 20 pieces at a quarter each. The day after that I bought and sold even more. What amazed me was that no one else caught on to the opportunity. More amazing was all the kids lining up to buy a piece of gum from me for a quarter when they could have bought an entire pack if they had just made the effort!

That summer, I was looking for another way to make some cash. My mother had paid me to pull weeds from the back yard, so now that I was a landscaping pro I ventured out to the neighborhood with my hoe and rake. I simply started knocking on doors asking my neighbors if they would like to be rid of their pesky weeds for only $1.25 an hour? At the time I had no idea how many doors I would have to knock on to make a sale or get an order. I simply wanted the results enough to go through the process, whatever it was.

When I did make a sale, I had to work my tail off in the Arizona heat to get paid. Before long I was looking for an easier way. One day while reading a comic book, I came across an ad for a business opportunity selling greeting cards. I ordered the package and waited.

A few weeks later my big box of cards showed up. I studied the sales manual for about an hour, picked up my sales kit, and hit the road. Believe it or not, I sold every last box of them, ordered another supply, and sold those, too. Don't ask me how many doors I had to knock on to find someone home, or how many people I had to actually pitch to in order to make a sale. I didn't count. I was young, inexperienced, and unconcerned. I read the manual, did what it said, and it worked. My enthusiasm and willingness to do the work made the "No's" a non-issue. It was certainly a lot easier to trade a box of cards for $5 than to spend hours in the sun weeding someone's yard to make the same profit!

A year or so later I found my next venture: address painting. I noticed one day that our house did not have the address painted on the curb, and neither did some of the others on our street. Recently,

Neighborhood Watch or some similar organization had distributed a flyer that suggested that house numbers be painted on the curb in front of your house for emergency and security reasons. I went to the local hardware store, bought a set of stencils, some masking tape, and a few cans of spray paint. I had everything I needed except, of course, customers. What did I do? You guessed it — up one side of the street, down the other. I showed the Neighborhood Watch flyer and offered to paint a nice set of white numbers on a black background on the curb for only $10.

Next came the Mother of All Kid Jobs – the paper route. My brother and I signed up for routes at the same time. Now this was work! We had to get up at the crack of dawn (or earlier) every morning — seven days a week — including holidays — and fold, rubber band, and bag our papers, cram them into our bike baskets and shoulder bags, then ride all over the neighborhood throwing the papers on doorsteps.

But that wasn't all. On afternoons and weekends we had to go "collecting," knocking on every customer's door and ask them to pay us for their subscription. We then paid the newspaper company their wholesale price for the papers, along with the cost of the rubber bands and bags. If what was left was not enough for us to be happy, we could always increase our earnings by increasing the number of subscriptions on our routes. That meant — you guessed it — up one side of the street and down the other knocking on doors trying to drum up more business.

This was probably one of the hardest jobs I ever had. Sure, I learned a lot and they say it builds character and responsibility, but compared to some of my previous ventures this one simply sucked. I hated getting up in the morning, the profit was minimal, and like the weeding venture, I had to do the sales, provide the grueling service, and collect the money. Throw in the fact that this was a 365-day-a-year job and I really wonder how I did it for a full year.

From toothpicks to bubble gum, greeting cards, yard work, address painting, and newspapers, the foundation was laid for my life in sales. Each of these ventures taught me that hard work and a lot of shoe leather were two factors for successful selling. I knew I was doing something different — more — than most other kids my age, but I wasn't giving it much thought at the time. It wasn't until my first "real" sales job that I learned there was much more to becoming successful. I discovered that becoming a success at selling, especially in the early stages of a sales career, is largely dependent on one's attitude, enthusiasm, and willingness to act rather than skill level. Selling truly is a numbers game. Those who succeed overcome their initial lack of experience with intense dedication and commitment backed by a positive attitude and tremendous enthusiasm for what they feel they must accomplish. Combine that attitude and enthusiasm with the willingness to follow a proven process for success and you have the foundation for a lifetime of success in selling! This book is about that proven sales process.

CHAPTER 1

HOW I WENT FROM ZERO TO SALES HERO IN 90 DAYS

I'll never forget my first "real" sales job. I was 22 years old and three days away from completing a two-week sales training program. I would soon be joining a team of 12 other "advertising consultants" selling display advertising in a weekly Pennysaver publication to local businesses. It was Wednesday, the day our new territories would be assigned. I had been doing very well in the class and I was excited to find out which one of the four available territories I would be awarded. To my shock and dismay, I was given Territory Seven, known among the existing staff as one of the "dog territories."

Territory Seven was famous for its string of failures. No sales rep had succeeded in Territory Seven. So why was I, the best candidate in the new class, being cursed with a territory in which I was sure to fail?

Jacqui, my trainer, manager, and soon-to-be mentor, saw my expression and laughed a little. She said, "Don, I'm giving you Territory Seven *because* you did well in the class...You have the right attitude and enthusiasm. That's a big part of what it takes to be successful. The salesperson determines the quality of the territory, not the other way around. Give it a month and let's see how it goes!" I agreed, reluctantly accepting that getting the "dog" was in some way a vote of confidence in my potential.

> The salesperson determines the quality
> of the territory, not the other way around.

That afternoon I decided to talk to the top two sales reps and ask for some advice on how best to succeed now that I was part of the team. Gary and Karina were in a class by themselves. They were consistently at the top performance levels, way above the rest of the sales team. I asked them both, "What do I need to do to get where you are?" Their answers were basically the same: "Just do exactly what you learned in the last two weeks." Huh? Surely these two had some secrets that helped them get so far ahead of the pack. Success couldn't be that simple. Why wouldn't everyone do what they learned in training? And if they did, why weren't they all as successful as Gary and Karina?

I would officially take over Territory Seven the following Monday. On Thursday and Friday, the last two days of training, I took every opportunity to talk with the other members of the team. It seemed that about half were moderately successful, and the other half were either failing or just getting by. Unlike Gary and Karina, these individuals had a lot to say. They had plenty of reasons for their lack of success:

I have a bad territory.

The product is not that good.

The accounting department is too strict and has cut off my clients.

My manager doesn't know what he's doing.

The economy is down.

Forget what you learned in training — they don't know what they're talking about. It sounds good in class but it doesn't work in the real world.

That was a lot to digest!

I went home for the weekend to get ready. Monday was coming and I was determined to be a success. I spent Saturday driving around my territory to get familiar with it and to map it out while writing down the names of a few dozen places that seemed like good prospects for my product.

I thought about what Gary and Karina said, and I thought about what all the others had said. Gary and Karina were outnumbered in their philosophies. There were many more team members on the "just getting by" side. However, Gary and Karina were making an awful lot of money. In fact, between them they were making more than everyone else combined!

It occurred to me that Gary and Karina attributed their success to their willingness and ability to follow proven success principles while the others' excuses pointed to everything *but* themselves. I made a personal commitment to follow the program I learned from Jacqui as closely as possible. In a way I was scared, but I couldn't wait to get going!

The day started, as usual, with the 8a.m. Monday sales meeting. Our publication was mailed every Tuesday, so the Monday morning meeting was followed by a full day of "cold calling." Jacqui had made it very clear that 80 percent of our success or failure was going to hinge on our willingness to make a lot of first-time calls on new potential customers. She told us that most salespeople hate to do it, and we spent a lot of time role playing and practicing so that we could overcome any hesitation and be as effective as possible. Personally, I didn't think it was a big deal and I knew I would have no problem with it. After all, didn't I do the same thing in all my ventures as a kid?

I drove to my territory, armed with the prospect list I created and a box full of sales materials. I was ready to go for it. All I needed to do was find a strip center or office complex, park the car, and walk in the first door. When I crossed the main street that was the boundary between Territory Four and Territory Seven, I found myself driving right by the first strip center — it just didn't look right. On down the road was another one but I didn't seem to notice it until I had passed it by. I finally pulled into the next one, and although there were plenty of potential customers there, I didn't see any on my list so I decided to move on.

I pulled into a convenience store to get a cup of coffee. I got back in my car, sipped the coffee, and tried to decide where to go next. I glanced at my watch — it was almost 11:00! I could no longer avoid the truth. I had to admit to myself that I was avoiding what I knew I had to do. But why? I knew what to do, I had done very well in practice, and I was in the middle of my territory with everything I needed at my disposal.

I was afraid.

That realization jolted me into action. I quickly drove to the next strip center, jumped out of the car, and sprinted through the first door before I could change my mind. "Hello, I'm Don Mastrangelo, can you tell me who handles your advertising?"

By lunchtime I had been through a dozen doors, collected about ten business cards, and had actually spoken with about three "decision makers." The remaining nine either were not in or were not willing to see me without an appointment. I soon found out that most of them were not going to give me an appointment, either! Of the three decision makers I did actually speak with, one was mildly interested, one completely shut me down saying he had tried our publication before and was unhappy with the results, and the third said "Not right now, but feel free to call me in a few months."

After lunch I went through another few dozen doors with similar results. At about four o'clock I finally drove back to the office. Jacqui sat down with me to review what I had done and was pleased. "Keep it up, Don, be consistent with this level of activity, and you will have more business than you can handle in a few months!" I sincerely hoped she was right!

Even Territory Seven had a handful of existing weekly advertisers, so on Tuesday and Wednesday I was able to enjoy a few breaks from the cold calling to service my new customers, delivering the current week's ad and finding out what changes the customer wanted to make for next week.

On Wednesday, something amazing happened. I was servicing an account, a roofing company that had been running an ad every week for years at a cost of $200 per week. The owner and I had been getting acquainted, and I had noticed in reviewing his file that each week he ran his ad in only one of our 30 zones (a zone was a geographic area covering about ten thousand households) that he apparently had determined were appropriate for his service. I happened to ask why he was running only one zone when he could get a 20-percent discount if he ran all three each week. Wouldn't the extra calls he was sure to get justify the additional expense?

He looked at me for a moment then told me that over a period of two years and after having at least four salespeople handle his account in that time I was the first to make him aware of that option. I tore up his weekly invoice for $200 and replaced it with one for $480, shook his hand, and said, "See you next week!" One simple question resulted in a 240-percent increase in weekly revenue for that account. Jacqui was very proud of that accomplishment and made a big deal out of it at the next Monday sales meeting.

THE FIRST SALE!

It was nine days before I finally made my first new sale! The "upsell" had been great, but it was nothing compared to the tremendous satisfaction of finding my own new customer. I found her on a cold call, a hair salon in the middle of my territory. The timing was right, the proprietor was looking for new business, and the product was a good fit. I wrote up a 13-week contract and accepted a check for Week One.

Over the next three months, motivated by these early successes, I maintained a furious pace and worked closely with my mentor. I had crammed a tremendous amount of work into a very short period of time. By the end of the third month I had created so much momentum that I could hardly keep up with it. I was making more money than I had ever expected and I was having the time of my life. However, most of my classmates were not doing so well. I could hear them talking with the other sales reps:

I have a bad territory.

The product is not that good.

The accounting department is too strict and has cut off my clients.

My manager doesn't know what he's doing.

The economy is down.

Forget what you learned in training — they don't know what they're talking about. It sounds good in class but it doesn't work in the real world.

> [I was making more money than I had ever expected
> and I was having the time of my life.]

THE COVETED "WORN OUT SHOE" AWARD

In one Monday sales meeting, Jacqui presented me with my first-ever sales award. To this day, no other honor or recognition has meant as much to me. It was a lapel pin in the shape of the sole of a shoe — with a hole in it. I wore it proudly. As far as I was concerned, Territory Seven was not such a "dog" after all.

I thoroughly enjoyed being at the top of my game when the inevitable happened — I was offered a promotion to regional sales manager! I would now have the opportunity to help a team of my own attain the same kind of success I had. The team I inherited was not doing very well, and it was going to be a challenge, but I knew I could do it. I would just share all my experience with them and they would be as successful as me! I conducted an intense training program that was based on what Jacqui had taught me, enhanced by a few of my own strategies that I had developed over the last few years. It was the start of the RSS System. I was sure that my team would be thrilled to get the information and put it to immediate use.

It did not take long for me to figure out that something was wrong. Only one of six team members was making substantial progress. It was Peter, who was the newest member and seemed eager to do whatever it would take to make it. For the rest nothing was changing. I couldn't understand why the sales weren't pouring in, so at the next sales meeting I went over the RSS System again to make sure everyone knew what to do. They all nodded enthusiastically so I was sure they had it this time. A few weeks later there was still no change. I brought each of them into my office for a one-on-one discussion. "What's happening out there? I'm not seeing the results I've been expecting. You're using the RSS System, right?"

Their responses were different, but also the same. They were not using the RSS System. Mark had his own ideas, Karen was having a hard time getting started. I wasn't all that surprised when later that day I overheard a few of my team members having a discussion:

I have a bad territory.

The product is not that good.

The accounting department is too strict and has cut off my clients.

My manager doesn't know what he's doing.

The economy is down.

Forget what you learned in training — they don't know what they're talking about. It sounds good in class but it doesn't work in the real world.

It was then that I learned what I believe is the most crucial truth about sales management. Until that day I believed that my job as a sales manager was to "make" my team successful. It became clear that I could not make anyone do anything if they did not want to do it. Rather, my job was to "require" each of my team members to become successful. I would provide a quality product, a positive sales environment, and all the training and support my team could handle. I would teach the RSS System to each new member of the team, but it was up to each individual to do his part. I met with each team member again and made it clear that following the RSS System was no longer an option. "If you follow this plan with a positive and enthusiastic attitude, you are likely to win. If you choose not to, you are likely to lose. It's your choice!"

> **I could not make anyone do anything
> if they did not want to do it.**

I started developing a simple activity tracking system so that each team member who was committed to success could track his own activity and hold himself accountable to the RSS System. It also gave me the ability to see who was and was not playing by the rules. The results were amazing. Those following the RSS System showed immediate and consistent sales growth. Those who did not did poorly and were either fired or quit. Each time I hired a new team member, I made it clear that an offer of employment was contingent on that individual's commitment to and demonstration of following the RSS System. For a short time, my turnover in team members was extremely high, but eventually I developed a truly successful sales team in which each member credited much of their success to making a personal choice to get from zero to sales hero in 90 days.

WHAT IT TAKES

Dedication, work ethic, commitment: Don't even think about a career in sales without these. Even after reading this book you will probably try to find a way around the simple, proven system I've laid out for you. If you become successful, it will be because at some point (I hope sooner than later) you will give up trying to find an "easier way" and will return to the RSS System.

Over the years I have put the RSS System behind everything I have done. I have built sales armies for several companies from the ground up. I have started, built, and sold companies of my own by basing our entire sales structure on the RSS System. I have experienced tremendous personal satisfaction in helping hundreds of individuals, most with no previous sales experience whatsoever, start successful sales careers. For almost 20 years, I have continually refined, tested, and updated the RSS System, but it remains essentially the same simple, proven program that helped me and countless others excel as both salespeople and sales managers.

> [**Dedication, work ethic, commitment:**
> **Don't even think about a career in sales without these.**]

The RSS System is a complete sales success system. You will start by setting personal and lifestyle objectives that translate to income objectives. Income objectives transition to sales objectives that transition to monthly, weekly, and daily action objectives for the first (or next) 90 days. You will devote considerable attention to tracking and understanding the results of that activity. Funnel and pipeline management, as well as forecasting, are also covered in detail.

I wrote this book for anyone who truly wants to get from zero to sales hero in 90 days. If you are new to sales, selling a new product, or have moved to a new company, you can guarantee your own success by making a personal commitment to following the RSS System. If you are a business owner who needs to personally sell your own product or service, read on. If you are a sales manager and need to turn your team around, you and your entire team need to read this book. If you run a large sales organization with an army of salespeople that needs to reach its goal, you will be amazed at how much better your pipeline will look in just a few short months once your entire organization is utilizing the RSS System!

CHAPTER 2

PARETO'S LAW
OR THE 80/20 RULE

There is a well-known rule in sales, commonly known as the 80/20 rule. In any sales organization 20 percent of the sales force will have 80 percent of the sales, while the other 80 percent of the sales force share the remaining 20 percent. I have personally witnessed the results of this "rule" as it has been proven over and over again across many organizations and sales applications. There is always a top 20 percent that make all the money!

> In any sales organization 20 percent of the sales force will have 80 percent of the sales.

Where did this rule come from? In fact, the 80/20 rule is not a rule, it's a "law." It comes from the work of Vilfredo Pareto, an eighteenth-century Italian economist. Pareto was only mildly influential during his lifetime, but his approach was resurrected and embraced during the great "Paretian Revival" of the 1930s and has guided much of modern economics since.

Pareto's Law has many applications that go far beyond the 80/20 rule as it pertains to sales. In any company, organization, government, or agency, 80 percent of the productivity will come from only 20 percent of the efforts. Eighty percent of the profits are produced by 20 percent of the employees. In a police force, 80 percent of the arrests are made by 20 percent of the officers. It can be applied another way: 20 percent of a business's customers create 80 percent of the problems. And so on.

Vilfredo Pareto, 1848-1923

Most important for you, Pareto's Law clearly mandates that 80 percent of your sales will be a result of only 20 percent of your efforts. The 20 percent of your efforts that lead to success is usually the part that nobody wants to do. So, you will naturally find yourself spending 80 percent of your time avoiding the 20 percent of the work that makes you money! This is especially true for the newest salesperson who simply does not know what to do or how to prioritize time. Meetings, crisis management, phone calls, office chat, paperwork, getting your ducks all lined up in a row are NOT part of the 20 percent of your activity that is directly attributable to creating new business. There is only one task proven to be *the* task that is *the* factor that is *the* 20 percent of activity that directly leads to achieving your sales objectives: *cold calling* or *prospecting*.

I have seen every possible attempt to find a way around Pareto's Law but none has succeeded. The only way to use this law to your advantage is to adopt an action plan that embraces the law rather than fights it. Once you accept the reality that you cannot change the rules of the numbers game, you will be able to make the decision simply to play by the rules or quit.

THE NUMBERS GAME

How many prospecting calls do you have to make? Let's apply Pareto's Law to find out. Let's say you decide to "complete" 100 prospecting calls in a given period of time. A completed call means that you actually spoke with the decision maker about your product or service to determine if he has an interest. According to

Pareto's Law, you will have had to walk through about five doors or made five phone attempts to actually reach one decision maker (20 percent of the total). Therefore, you will make 500 attempts to attain your goal of completing 100 prospecting calls.

Of the 100 decision makers you actually spoke with, 20 (20 percent) are going to have a genuine interest and will stay in the game — your pipeline — for further follow up, while 80 (80 percent), no matter how good at selling you are or how much you know they need what you have to offer, are simply not going to be interested — they are *out* of the game.

Now, through appointments, proposals, and follow-up calls, you will find that 80 percent (or 16) of the 20 prospects that were still IN the game are not going to buy (at least not right now), for whatever reason. There is absolutely nothing you can do about it. They are *out* of the game for now. It's not you, it's the law. Don't worry, they may get back *in* the game later!

That leaves four decision makers who buy your product! Congratulations, you just made your first four sales! At first this may seem like small reward for all your efforts, but you will learn that it is a good, solid formula that will help you get from zero to sales hero in 90 days!

The Buying Cycle

The "Buying Cycle," shown in Figure 1, is another way to illustrate how Pareto's Law affects your sales efforts:

Figure 1. The Buying Cycle

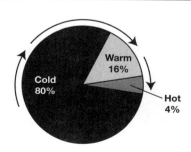

Assuming once again that you complete 100 prospecting calls, let's classify the outcome of each completed call as "cold," "warm," or "hot." The results will consistently be:

COLD	80%	Not Interested
WARM	16%	Interested
HOT	4%	Very Interested

Notice that 80 percent are not interested (cold); 20 percent are at least interested enough to give you an appointment or the opportunity to make a presentation (warm and hot). Of the 20 percent that are interested, 20 percent of those are very interested or likely to buy *now* (hot).

The buying cycle constantly changes. Those who are "hot" today will probably buy your product. If a competitor shows up next week to complete a prospecting call on the same prospect, his result will be "cold" because your new customer is no longer in the market for the product or service just obtained from you. Similarly, if one of your prospects was "warm" last week and yesterday had a negative experience with his current provider, he may be "hot" today!

Prospects will continually move from "cold" to "warm" to "hot" as their needs and experiences change. If you call on the same 100 prospects six months later the percentages will be the same but the names will be different — you will never run out of potential buyers! Figure 2 represents the typical results of 100 completed prospecting calls:

Figure 2. 100 Typical Prospecting Calls

COLD	COLD	COLD	**WARM**	COLD	COLD	COLD	**WARM**	COLD	COLD
COLD	**WARM**	COLD	**WARM**	COLD	**HOT**	COLD	COLD	COLD	COLD
COLD	COLD	COLD	COLD	COLD	**WARM**	COLD	**WARM**	COLD	**WARM**
COLD	COLD	COLD	COLD	COLD	COLD	COLD	COLD	COLD	COLD
WARM	COLD	COLD	COLD	COLD	**HOT**	COLD	COLD	COLD	**WARM**
COLD	**WARM**	COLD	COLD	COLD	COLD	COLD	COLD	COLD	COLD
COLD	COLD	**WARM**	COLD	COLD	COLD	**WARM**	COLD	COLD	COLD
COLD	**WARM**	COLD	COLD	COLD	**HOT**	COLD	COLD	COLD	COLD
COLD	COLD	COLD	**HOT**	COLD	COLD	**WARM**	COLD	COLD	COLD
COLD	COLD	COLD	COLD	COLD	**WARM**	COLD	COLD	**WARM**	COLD

This is a great representation of how prospecting calls "feel" in the field or on the phone. Let's assume you are on the phone calling prospects from a list you obtained. If you were not aware of Pareto's Law you might have become very discouraged early on. In fact, based on Figure 2 you did not find a "hot" prospect until your 16th completed prospecting call, and you didn't find your second hot prospect until you completed your 46th call! What was going through your mind as you got through to decision maker after decision maker only to hear dozens of "No's" and "Maybe's"? It might have been very difficult to maintain your positive attitude and enthusiasm!

But you were empowered with the knowledge of Pareto's Law! You knew that 80 percent of the decision makers you reached would say "No." You were prepared that 16 would be warm or at least mildly interested. And you knew that there were at least four hot prospects out there to be found — it was almost fun to go through the 100 possibilities to identify your warm and hot prospects. And now you have 20 warm and hot prospects in your pipeline! Way to get started!

CHAPTER

THE SALES FUNNEL AND PIPELINE

To manage your sales activity effectively, it is extremely important to understand how to continually monitor your sales "funnel," "pipeline," and "forecast." Using Figure 3, you can see how the sales funnel and pipeline help you manage your sales activity based on Pareto's Law:

Figure 3. Sales Funnel, Pipeline, and Forecast

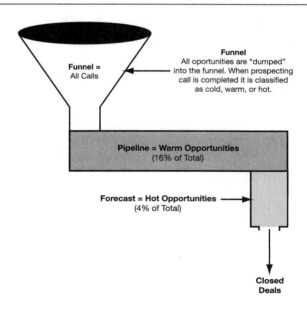

First, all of your prospects — or potential customers — are "dumped" into the funnel. As you complete prospecting calls to decision makers, you will initially qualify them as cold (80 percent), warm (16 percent), or hot (4 percent).

> It is extremely important to understand how to continually monitor your sales "funnel," "pipeline," and "Forecast."

The prospects classified as cold do not make it past the funnel into the pipeline. Your warm and hot prospects make it past the funnel and start to flow through the pipeline. These are the opportunities that will either "close" or fall through in the near future. A closed sale is a completed sale — you have a signed order and a check, if applicable. At least 20 percent of the prospects in your pipeline, or 4 percent of the total completed prospecting calls *will* close within a reasonable time. Some will close immediately and some will take time. Others will not close and will need to be purged from the pipeline. Don't fight it; it's the law and you can't change it. It's better to understand and embrace the reality that you simply need to continually fill the funnel with enough prospecting activity to give you the results you want. Controlling the amount of prospecting activity you do keeps you in control of the end results. You can always count on closing *at least* 4 percent of what you put in the funnel!

THE READY, SET, SELL! SYSTEM

SETTING PERSONAL GOALS AND OBJECTIVES

THE ULTIMATE CUSTOMER PROFILE

PROSPECTING CALLS

RELATIONSHIP SELLING: THE APPOINTMENT

MANAGING YOUR PIPELINE AND FORECAST

HOW TO WIN THE NUMBERS GAME

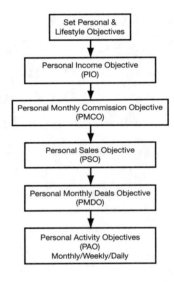

CHAPTER 4

PERSONAL GOALS AND OBJECTIVES

What will inspire you to do what it takes to become part of the top 20 percent? To play the game and win, you'll need to know exactly why you are playing.

When things get tough, and they always do, you will need a compelling reason to keep going. When you reach a crossroads and find yourself struggling, you will either drop the ball or keep running. It is your personal goals and objectives that will inspire you to stay in the game. If your personal objectives are strong enough, you will break through any barrier that gets in your way.

Setting goals is absolutely essential. However, only 20 percent of all salespeople do it. Further, only 20 percent of those who do have a clear idea of what they want and write their goals down! Over the years, I have witnessed that the 4 percent of all salespeople out there who have precise, written goals achieve more than the other 96 percent combined! Success is truly a matter of choice.

THE RSS SYSTEM

To begin, you will create your personal objectives in three major steps:

Step 1. Lifestyle and Income Objective

Step 2. Personal Sales Objective (PSO)

Step 3. Personal Activity Objective (PAO)

STEP 1. Lifestyle and Income Objectives

The first step is unquestionably the most important for the other steps are based on what you do here. Some of your personal objectives will be financially based, others will require a change in lifestyle or available leisure time. For example, one of your personal goals might be to purchase a new home. To attain that goal, you will have a monthly goal equal to the monthly payment. Another goal may be to spend more time with a hobby, which requires flexibility of time. Although the process of setting your goals and objectives will be primarily centered around finances, it is also important to include lifestyle objectives in your overall plan.

The first step is to write down the things you need to spend money on every month. Start with the basic items, such as your rent or mortgage, utilities, food, entertainment, clothing, credit card and loan payments, car payments, insurance, and so on. If your objectives include a more expensive home or car, write in the higher amount. If you would like to reduce or eliminate debt, increase the monthly amount you will pay on credit cards and other loans so that they can be reduced or eliminated within the time frame you set. Wherever possible, break each item down to a monthly cost.

In addition to the basic items, try to write down five to ten things that you would really like to do, see, experience, or have. Include travel and vacations, hobbies and interests, competitions, sports, music, writing, and other such items. Other things that may inspire you could include donations to your church and/or charities, spending more time with loved ones, or volunteering your time in any number of worthwhile and rewarding ways. Again, try to break everything down to a monthly cost. For example, if one of your objectives is to take a yearly all-inclusive family vacation at a cost of $5,000, your monthly cost for this item is just over $400.

Once you have written down everything you want to have and achieve and it's corresponding monthly cost, you can identify your monthly net income objective. If you haven't already, now would be a good time to include an objective of setting aside some of your income for investments. Your investment advisor can help you determine the appropriate percentage. Next, include a "buffer" of around 5 percent to cover miscellaneous items and minor things you have not considered.

Finally, take your monthly net income objective and add enough to cover your personal taxes. The final number is your monthly Personal Income Objective (PIO).

Congratulations — you have just made your first and most important move toward becoming a winner. You are one step closer to joining the top 20 percent!

It is important to keep your goals in front of you as often as possible. A fun way to do this is to create a collage of photos, messages, and so on, that remind you of what is important to you. Make a large one to hang on your wall. Make a small one that you can insert in your planner or portfolio. If you find yourself out in the field thinking about "dropping the ball," reach for your objectives and let them inspire you to keep going!

As with everything, things will change in your life and career. You can and should reset your short-term goals when you need to. Sometimes they will get bigger and sometimes smaller. If you find that your goals are currently completely out of reach, don't hesitate to reduce them to an attainable level. Just make sure you are always stretching to achieve more until you get where you really want to be!

Okay, you know how much money you *need* to make. The next step is to determine how much of your product or service you need to sell so that you can consistently achieve your PIO.

STEP 2. Personal Sales Objective (PSO)

To convert your PIO to your Personal Sales Objective (PSO), you will need a thorough understanding of your compensation plan. Some positions provide a base salary plus commissions, while others are "commission only." Don't be afraid of commission-only plans — they usually offer unlimited earning potential! Some plans pay a commission based on a percentage of actual sales, while others pay a per unit sales commission.

Begin by writing down your monthly PIO. If your compensation plan includes a base salary, subtract it from the PIO. The remaining amount is the net monthly commission you need to earn to reach your PIO. Add in enough to cover taxes and withholding on your commissions to determine your Personal Monthly Commission Objective (PMCO).

For example:

Base Salary Plus Commission

PIO	$4,000
Minus Base Salary	- $2,000
Net Monthly Commission	$2,000
Plus Withholding Taxes	+ $175
PMCO	$2,175

Commission Based on a Percentage of Actual Sales

If you are paid a commission based on a percentage of actual sales, the next step is to divide the PMCO by the commission percentage you are paid. This will result in your PSO. For example, if you earn a commission of 15 percent of gross sales, your PSO will be $14,500:

PMCO	$2,175
Divided By Commission	÷ 15%
PSO	$ 14,500

Personal Monthly Deals Objective (PMDO)

Now you can determine your actual Personal Monthly Deals Objective (PMDO). Divide your PSO by the average revenue per sale or "deal" at your organization. In this case let's assume the average revenue per deal is $725. You will need to close 20 deals per month:

PSO	$ 14,500
Divided By Revenue per Deal	÷ $725
PMDO	20

Per Unit Compensation

If your compensation plan is based on a per unit commission, you can determine your PSO simply by dividing your PMCO by the average commission earned per unit. For example, if the average commission is $75 per unit sold, you will need to sell 29 units per month to reach your PIO:

PMDO	$2,175
Divided By Average Commission per Unit	÷ $75
PSO	29

To calculate your PMDO, divide your PSO by the average number of units per deal. For example, if your sales organization averages six units per deal, your PMDO will be five:

PSO (Units)	29
Divided By Average Units per Deal Sold	÷ 6
PMDO	5

STEP 3. Personal Activity Objective (PAO)

Are you ready to learn exactly what you have to do in the next 90 days? With a firm grasp on your PIO and PSO, let's apply Pareto's Law to determine exactly how much prospecting activity – your Personal Activity Objective (PAO) — will be required to reach your desired lifestyle!

We already know that 20 percent of the decision makers you reach will have some interest and 20 percent of those (or roughly 4 percent of your completed prospecting calls) will result in a sale of your product or service sooner than later.

If you are paid a commission based on a percentage of actual sales, following through on our earlier example, we have determined that your PMDO is 20. Since 20 is 4 percent of 500, your monthly PAO is 500, your weekly PAO is 125, and your daily PAO is 25, assuming you work a typical five-day work week:

PMDO	20
Divided by 4 Percent	÷ 4%
Monthly PAO	500
Divided by Four Weeks	÷ 4
Weekly PAO	125
Divided by Five Days per Week	÷ 5
Daily PAO	25

If your compensation plan is based on a per unit commission, again following through on our earlier example, we have determined that your PMDO is five. Five is 4 percent of 125, so your monthly PAO is 125, your weekly PAO is 32, and your daily PAO is six:

PMDO	5
Divided by Four Percent	÷ 4%
Monthly PAO	125
Divided by Four Weeks	÷ 4
Weekly PAO	32
Divided by Five Days per Week	÷ 5
Daily PAO	6

Remember that your PAOs are always based on "completed" prospecting calls in which you have actually reached a decision maker and determined if they are cold, warm, or hot. On average, your completed prospecting calls will be 20 percent of your actual prospecting attempts. The decision maker may not be in or cannot (or will not) see you. You might not get past the "gatekeeper" or you got the decision maker's voice mail. Whatever the reason, 80 percent of your prospecting call attempts will result in a call that could not be completed. So if your Daily PAO is six, you will need to make approximately 30 attempts each day to attain your PAO. How long does an attempt take? It will vary, but consider that on an attempt — rather than a completed prospecting call — you are speaking with someone other than the decision maker and gathering some basic information about the company, the decision maker, his availability, and so on. Depending on whether you are making your attempts by phone or by walking through doors, each will require only a few minutes at most. Therefore, 30 attempts should take between 30 and 90 minutes, which, not surprisingly, is equal to about 20 percent of your eight-hour day — Pareto strikes again!

Your daily PAO is by far your highest priority. Get it done first and you will still have 80 percent of your day available for whatever else needs to be done.

> STOP right here and determine your monthly, weekly, and daily PAO before reading on!

Refer to the goal-setting worksheet (page 75), which will take you through the entire goal-setting process.

DECIDE TO WIN!

Are you excited? I hope you are! You are much better prepared to succeed now than you were when you started reading this book. You should now know exactly what you want and when you want it. You should have set your Personal Income Objective, Personal Sales Objective, and Personal Activity Objective and know exactly what you have to do each day for the next 90 days. In fact, you *know* that if you follow the RSS System for the next 90 days you *will* achieve your goals — you *will* win the game!

However, even after learning how the game works, only 20 percent of you will actually play to win! It has nothing to do with your past experience, the product or service you sell, or the company you represent. It makes no difference that you do or don't have a college degree. It doesn't matter how old or young you are, who your manager is, or how the economy is doing. It simply comes down to this:

- Are you ready to make the decision that you absolutely will achieve your goals no matter what obstacles get in your way?

- Are you truly and sincerely committed to achieving success?

- Are your goals important enough to inspire you to do what you need to do, when you need to do it, whether you feel like it or not?

- Do you believe that if you make a personal commitment to following the RSS System for the next 90 days, that you really will win?

By following the RSS System, *you will win*! I have *never* seen anyone who followed the RSS System with a positive attitude and enthusiasm fail. Don't get me wrong, I've seen plenty of sales reps go through the motions for a while and quit. In fact, the only way you can lose is to quit before you get the job done. If you are committed to winning, have a positive attitude, are enthusiastic, and follow the rules for at least three consecutive months, you will win!

> **The only way you can lose
> is to quit before you get the job done.**

I sincerely hope that you will become one of the success stories. Just think: In the next 90 days you can lay the groundwork for a lifetime of success and achievement. In just three months *you* could be joining the Top 20 Percent Club! You now have everything you need at your disposal. All you have to do is make the decision to win! Repeat the following statement out loud until you absolutely believe it:

> **I have made the decision that I absolutely will achieve
> my goals no matter what obstacles get in my way!**

CHAPTER 5

THE ULTIMATE CUSTOMER PROFILE

Now that you have made the decision to succeed, it's time to determine who to call on. You have a daily, weekly, and monthly PAO that requires you to complete prospecting calls to new decision makers each day. Where do you start?

You may have access to a list of your organization's past or dormant customers, or you could just start driving around looking for prospects that may need your product or service. A better idea may be to pick up the local Yellow Pages or to purchase a list of prospects from a reputable supplier of such information.

Regardless, start by creating a profile of your ultimate prospect. Ask your manager, mentor, or marketing department for assistance. If you sell primarily to other businesses, are there certain types of companies that buy what you sell more often than others? Are larger or smaller companies more likely to buy? What about geography — do you have the ability to sell anywhere or do you need to focus on a certain territory?

If you sell to individuals rather than to businesses, are there other criteria to consider? Is your ultimate prospect married or single? Male or female? Does your prospect have children? What is the average age of your most likely buyer? Does she own or rent? What is her income level? Is the type of car she drives relevant?

> Visit us on the web at www.donmastrangelo.com
> for links to reputable providers of business and
> residential leads and prospecting lists.

CHAPTER

PROSPECTING CALLS

This is it — you are ready to go! You have clear objectives, you have made the decision to win, and you have your list of prospects that fit your Ultimate Customer Profile. Let's get started!

OBJECTIVES

There are three objectives of the prospecting call:

1. Make a great first impression.

2. Find out who the decision maker is.

3. If possible, determine whether the prospect is cold, warm, or hot.

Make a Great First Impression

Your prospects are exposed to a lot of salespeople. You'll want to differentiate yourself from the pack. You should be positive, professional, and courteous, but also confident and enthusiastic. Remember, you know you have something of value to offer. Whether this prospect is open to what you are presenting is beyond your control, but you can always control your attitude and enthusiasm!

Find Out Who the Decision Maker Is

If the decision maker is unavailable, make sure that you find out who he is, and make sure you make a great first impression with the person you talk to. Leave behind some information and ask that it be given to the decision maker. If you have made a favorable impression on the "gatekeeper" or receptionist, the chances of your material being delivered increases dramatically, as does the probability that the decision maker will accept your call when you follow up.

Determine Whether the Prospect Is Cold, Warm, or Hot
Remember, 80 percent of the prospecting calls you make will be to decision makers who for whatever reason simply do not perceive a need for what you have to offer at this time. They are cold — let them go! Remember the buying cycle? There is a good chance these prospects will — in their time, not yours — become warm or hot. By making the best first impression you can, the door will be open for you to continue checking in and be ready to help them when they are ready.

What to Say and Do in a Prospecting Call

Keep it simple. You are not there to tell anyone who will listen everything there is to know about you, your product or service, or your company. Don't let yourself come off like the smooth talker or pushy closer!

With confidence and controlled enthusiasm, simply introduce yourself, state your purpose, and ask who you would need to talk to about your product or service. Ask if that person might happen to be available. If not, leave your information, ask that it be forwarded, and ask the person you have been speaking with when a good time would be for you to contact the decision maker. If he is available, start with a brief introduction of yourself and your product, and try to include a common benefit. Always finish your introduction with an open-ended question that will require your prospect to think and respond, initiating a dialogue (See example below).

Recently I served as director of sales for a wonderful company that sold a global positioning system (GPS) fleet management solution for companies that employed a mobile work force. While there I had the opportunity use the RSS System (of course) to build both direct sales and dealer channels for the company. The solution we were selling allowed owners or fleet managers of a company to virtually "ride with every driver all day every day" by installing a GPS-equipped box in each of their fleet vehicles. The box would keep track of every stop the vehicle made, including the address and cross street, how long the vehicle was stopped, time and distance between stops, the route taken between stops, and so on. The dispatcher and/or fleet manager could log on to his account and see everything that was happening historically and in near real-time. The benefits of implementing this solution usually included, one or all of the following:

- Reduced miles driven on the vehicles
- Reduced overtime
- Improved dispatching
- Increased jobs/stops/deliveries
- Reduced maintenance costs
- Improved customer service

Shown below is an example of a typical prospecting call introduction that was used by the sales force for this company. Let's assume that the salesperson (you) is calling a prospect who is president of ABC Courier Service, a company with 20 or so employees making deliveries and pick-ups in a mid-sized metropolitan area:

You: *Hello, [prospect's name]. This is [your name] with The GPS Company. Are you familiar with how a GPS fleet solution can help your business?*

Prospect: *(No or Yes)*

You: *Basically what we do is help you to save money by reducing miles driven on your vehicles, reducing unnecessary overtime, and increasing the number of stops/jobs/deliveries that can be accomplished by your fleet. How many vehicles are in your fleet?*

Here are some examples of typical cold, warm, and hot responses that our salespeople would get:

Scenario #1: C-C-COLD!

Prospect: *You know, all of our vehicles are owned by the employees and they are independent contractors. We've looked at a system such as yours and determined that we simply do not want or need it.*

This is a typical cold response. The customer has checked into such a system in the past and decided there is no need. Is the decision maker wrong? Probably. The salesperson knows it because she has helped similar companies save money and increase efficiency.

The salesperson will try to overcome this "objection" with a response such as:

You: *I understand your employees are independent contractors and you don't see a way to save money on reduced miles or overtime. Do you find that you sometimes dispatch a courier from across town only to later determine you had another courier available that was five miles closer?*

Prospect: *Well, sure that sometimes happens.*

You: *Our system would have allowed you to dispatch the closer courier, which would have a substantial impact on your efficiency, and could increase the number of pick-ups and deliveries you get done in a day. There are many other ways we can help you decrease costs and increase efficiency, and I'd be happy to discuss them with you. When can we meet?*

Nice job! And it will sometimes work! However, in this case the prospect says, "I see where you're going, but we looked at all the possibilities and we are just not interested at this time. Thanks for calling and have a nice day."

The salesperson did a good job, and with your growing experience, product knowledge, and confidence you will get better at taking the prospecting call as far as you can, overcoming objections whenever possible. But in the end, you can only control how you handle the call, not the decision maker's response or the outcome of the call. Pareto's Law says that 80 out of 100 completed prospecting calls will result in a "No." They are cold. Make a note to call them back in a few months and move on.

Scenario #2: You're Getting WARMER

Here's an example of a call where the response is more positive:

Prospect: *Well, we have about 20 vehicles. How is your system going to save us money on overtime?*

You: *Let me ask you this: How do your employees clock in and out?*

Prospect: *They keep a time card with them and they write down the time they start and stop.*

You: *Have you ever had concerns that this timekeeping is not completely accurate?*

Prospect: *Sure we have. Our employees clock in when they leave their homes in the morning and clock out when they leave their last job of the day. We know there is some abuse.*

You: *With our solution you will know exactly when your employees leave their homes for work and when they leave the last job of the day, eliminating any abuse. There are many other benefits, which I would be happy to discuss with you in person.*

Prospect: *Tell you what: I can't promise anything, but you are welcome to come and tell me more.*

You: *Great! I'll be near your office this Thursday morning. Would 9 o'clock or 11 o'clock be better for you?*

The outcome of this call is warm. The decision maker is interested. He certainly has not made a commitment to buy, but the prospect knew he had some issues with overtime and the salesperson was able to peak his interest enough to get an appointment to take the discussion further! On the average, this will happen on 16 out of every 100 completed prospecting calls. Add this prospect to your pipeline and continue to follow up until his status turns to hot or cold.

Scenario #3: HOT! HOT! HOT!

Okay, you earned it! Here is an example of a hot prospect:

Prospect: *You know, it's funny that you called today! Last weekend I was in Las Vegas at our annual convention and one of my peers gave a talk about how he implemented your solution and put an extra $20,000 in his pocket last year by cutting overtime and side jobs. Come and see me — I want to know more!*

Wow, doesn't that feel great? The salesperson is excited! This is a hot prospect. The prospect knows he has a need and he wants to fix it. You can count on this outcome in four out of every 100 completed prospecting calls. These are the peaks that help keep you going through the valleys (4 percent = hot). Add this prospect to your forecast and go for the close!

Those decision makers who express a genuine interest in learning more about your product or service (warm and hot) will progress from your funnel to your pipeline or forecast. Those who are not interested at this time (cold) do not! Don't make this more complicated than it is. I am always amazed at how reluctant most salespeople are to let a cold prospect go. Yes, you need a certain number of prospects in your pipeline, but you will only fool yourself and waste valuable time if you are not completely honest with yourself. As you develop your selling skills, you will learn to overcome objections and to "dig deeper" in the prospecting call. However, your percentage of cold, warm, and hot won't change significantly. Hey, it's the LAW!

THREE STRIKES AND **THEY'RE OUT!**

If you were not able to complete the prospecting call, you should wait until the next day and try to reach the decision maker again. If you get through, use the same introduction. Again, *only* after speaking with the decision maker will you be able to determine whether this prospect is cold, warm, or hot. If you do not get through on your first attempt, leave your message and consider that Strike One for this prospect. Try again the next day. If the decision maker is out or does not take your call, that's Strike Two. He gets one more chance to find out how you can help him.

After three attempts to reach the decision maker without success, you can usually assume that the prospect is not interested and just doesn't want to talk with you. This isn't always the case, but it is better to write him off and keep prospecting than to continue trying to get through to someone who is just not interested. This

Figure 4. Three Strikes and THEY'RE OUT!

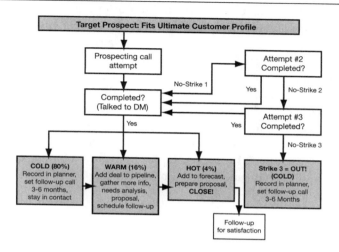

prospect is *cold — move on!* You are not trying to make prospects something that they are not. Three strikes and they're *out!*

TRACKING COMPLETED PROSPECTING CALLS

It is extremely important to track your prospecting call activity and the results. See Chapter 11, "Tracking Your Sales Activity," for how to do this.

KEEP A "TICKLER FILE" FOR FOLLOW-UP CALLS

You are obviously investing a tremendous amount of time and energy in calling prospects, and your highest priority is to achieve your daily PAO to find warm and hot prospects to fill your pipeline. However, you are also meeting and making a great first impression on dozens, if not hundreds, of qualified but currently cold prospects along the way that, because of their present position in the buying cycle, are simply not yet ready to buy your product or service. Your "tickler file" provides a method to keep adequate notes on your past sales activity with your prospects. It is also a great way for you to remind yourself to contact cold prospects at a later date to determine if they have migrated from cold to warm or hot. Finally, the tickler file will help you manage your current sales activity relating to the warm and hot prospects that make up your pipeline and follow-up activities on your current customers, if applicable.

Your tickler file can be as simple as an entry for a future date in your planner or calendar or an electronic reminder in your customer relationship management (CRM) software. Regardless of the method you choose, consistent use of a tickler file will ensure that you don't let the efforts you have invested today in the identification of a potential future opportunity slip through the cracks. See Chapter 11 for an example of how to keep track of your activity with each prospect and current customer.

Chapter

Relationship Selling:
The Appointment

So, you have identified a warm or hot prospect that is ready for a presentation or appointment. What do you do when you get there? Your objective is to uncover one or more specific needs the prospect has that can be satisfied with your product or service. These needs may not be apparent on the surface. The prospect may not just volunteer the information. You will need to look for it. When you have found a specific need you can sell directly to it.

Relationship selling is also known as "needs-based" selling, "SPIN selling" (Situation, Problem, Implication, Need-Payoff), and "NIS" (Needs Integrated Selling).

Key Components of a Relationship Selling Appointment

The following outline shows the key components of a "relationship selling" appointment:

1. Introduce your Product

2. Ask probing questions

3. Listen for the implied need

4. Test the need for importance to the Customer

5. Satisfy the need

Let's look at these points individually.

Introduce Your Product

Your first goal is to enter into a dialogue with the customer. You need to get down to business within just a few minutes out of respect for the prospect's time. Introduce yourself and ask a question or two about the person or business:

You: *How long has ABC Courier been in business? How did you come to own the business? Did you start it from scratch or buy it?*

It is an accepted fact that people love to talk about themselves and about what they do, but are rarely given the opportunity. Become a good listener, and as the prospect opens up, continue asking "open-ended" questions that expand on what the prospect tells you.

Prospect: *I started it myself as a one-man-show and built it to 20 vehicles over the last ten years.*

You: *What was your greatest challenge?*

The prospect will subconsciously think of you as a smart, helpful individual because you took a sincere interest in what they had to say and listened more than talked.

Ask Probing Questions

Now that you have some basic information on the individual and you have made a good impression, it's time to find out more about your prospect's history in regard to your product or service:

You: *On the phone you mentioned you believe there is some abuse when it comes to overtime hours. How is that affecting your business?*

Listen For the Implied Need

Your probing questions will help you to get information that you can use to your benefit. Listen for an opening and expand on it with further open-ended questions:

Prospect: *We're paying about five hours a week per courier in overtime.*

You: *If you could ride with every driver every day, how much of that could you eliminate?*

Prospect: *I think we could cut out at least two hours per courier per week.*

Test the Need for Importance to the Customer

A common mistake is to attempt to close based on an implied need only to find out that this need was not very important to the prospect. You should test the need. Use a closed probing question (requiring a "yes" or "no" answer) to test your implied need:

You: *If I could show you how our system could help you cut two hours of overtime per courier, would that be enough to eliminate your overtime problem?*

Prospect: *Yes. If you can save us even one hour of overtime per courier per week with your system, we'll be very pleased with the results.*

Satisfy the Need

When you have uncovered a need (or needs), tested it, and found that the customer considers it important and wants to fix the problem, CLOSE! Determine how your product or service can be tailored to fit the need and present your solution to the prospect. Only sell benefits that directly satisfy the need:

You: *Great, our system will allow you to virtually be "with" each of your driver's every day. You've stated that with that ability you are sure you could cut two hours of overtime per day, and that even saving one hour would be satisfactory. Let's get you started!*

The process of relationship selling is simple: Ask a lot of questions — and listen! Let the prospect do the talking. Think of it as a tennis match — you can't plan a return shot until the other player hits the ball. You should not know what you are going to say next until after the prospect finishes what he is saying. You won't master this overnight. It will take practice.

Don't put too much pressure on yourself here. Relationship selling is reserved for an appointment. You will not have an appointment unless you are dealing with a warm or hot prospect. That means the prospect has a need, knows it, and is at least interested enough to agree to a meeting with you. Believe me, there is a need to be fulfilled and all you have to do is find it.

The decision maker would prefer that you ask these questions and sell to his need rather than have you spew out everything you know about your product in hopes that he will let you know when you've hit on something. As you start putting relationship selling into practice, you will naturally improve and so will your closing ratio.

There are many techniques you can learn to enhance your skills in relationship selling, including books and tapes available on the subject. Visit our website at *www.donmastrangelo.com* for the most up-to-date list.

CHAPTER 8

MANAGING YOUR PIPELINE AND FORECAST

You will stay in touch with the cold prospects that fit your "Ultimate Customer Profile" through your tickler file, but your pipeline includes only your warm and hot prospects. As you start accumulating warm and hot prospects in your pipeline, you will need to be able to keep track of which opportunities are likely to close in your current and future sales cycles.

THE PIPELINE

You will want to know what stage each deal in your pipeline is in and upgrade or downgrade the stage as the opportunity progresses. For example, let's assume you have a prospect that is classified as cold from a prospecting call several months ago. You make a follow-up or tickler file call and you are pleased to find that based on recent events the decision maker is now warm! You will change the rating for this prospect from cold to warm, adding it to your pipeline. Likewise, if a warm opportunity in your pipeline deteriorates, it should be downgraded to cold, removing the opportunity from your pipeline until circumstances change. Again, only your warm and hot prospects make up your pipeline. Obviously, the larger your pipeline the more deals you will close.

The Forecast

You (and your manager and her manager, and so on up the chain) will want to be able to determine which deals are likely to close within a given time. This is the purpose of your "forecast." The forecast should only include hot prospects or deals — those that are very likely to close within your current sales cycle. The goal is to allow you and your organization to accurately forecast or estimate how much business you will close based on which opportunities in your pipeline are at the stage of hot. If a hot opportunity deteriorates, downgrade it to warm or cold as appropriate. If this opportunity is downgraded to warm, it will remain in the pipeline but not the forecast. If the downgrade is to cold, the prospect can remain in your tickler file but is no longer in the pipeline.

Your organization could have a weekly, monthly, or quarterly forecast, or any combination of these. Most important is that you accurately forecast what you will actually close in the given sales cycle. Your managers will appreciate your accuracy in forecasting.

An interesting fact: Once you have been following the RSS System for a few months, you will find that at any given time your tickler file, which includes your entire universe of cold, warm, or hot prospects, will consistently include 80 percent cold prospects, 16 percent warm prospects, and 4 percent hot prospects — regardless of the total number of prospects you have called on since starting!

CHAPTER

HOW TO WIN "THE NUMBERS GAME"

As a general rule, you will know that you have won The Numbers Game when you begin to feel the *momentum* kick in. You have paid the price of investing a tremendous amount of activity into a relatively short amount of time. You suddenly have more deals in the pipeline with less effort. It's getting easier to get those deals closed. You seem to have more confidence in yourself and your product or service. It's like you have been riding a bicycle up a steep hill, have crested the top, and are beginning to enjoy the rush of the cool air as you coast down the other side.

> **You will know that you have won The Numbers Game when you begin to feel the MOMENTUM kick in.**

Suddenly, the last few months don't seem like they were that difficult after all! You are making great money and earning respect and recognition from your entire organization — you did it! You went from Zero to Sales Hero in 90 days!

It's too bad so many others stopped during the climb. While you are enjoying the thrill of accomplishment, they are frustrated, disappointed, and broke!

Managing Your Momentum

Over the last 90 days, you were spending the majority of your time completing prospecting calls to new decision makers. You invested 80 percent of your efforts accomplishing your most important objective: Your PAO. You did not dare get distracted from that incredibly important process. You made sure that you did not allow all the non-prospecting activities that needed to be done to take up more than 20 percent of your time — well done!

Now that you have gone from zero to sales hero in 90 days, you will find that you can — and must — shift your focus. You have so much activity in your pipeline that you will now be spending a considerable amount of time on appointments, presentations, proposals, follow-up calls, and so on. In most cases, you will find that you will now need to invest only 20 percent of your time completing prospecting calls to keep the pipeline full and to consistently close enough business to reach your PSO. Never stop prospecting! If you do, your pipeline will get very thin and you will have to start the process all over again!

[**Never stop prospecting!**]

Imagine you get a flat tire on your car. Unfortunately, you realize that your spare is flat, too. You decide to forget the spare for now and just roll the flat to the station for repair. After struggling to lift the wheel upright from the ground, you start rolling it toward the station. It takes considerable effort to get it going. The wheel wobbles and goes all over the place at first but after a while it just rolls along in the direction you point it with little effort. After a short distance you can just walk along beside it and give it an occasional tap. What happens if you stop tapping? The tire rolls along just fine for a while, then it starts wobbling erratically again and eventually falls down to the same position it was in when you started. Now you have to start all over again!

If you consistently invest at least 20 percent of your time completing prospecting calls and filling the pipeline you will always have *momentum* on your side!

REFERRALS

Referrals from satisfied customers are one of the best — and least utilized — sources for new business opportunities. While prospecting, you should always ask for referrals regardless of whether the prospect was cold, warm, or hot. If you have just completed a prospecting call in which your prospect was cold, simply try this:

You: *I respect that you have decided my product is not right for you at this time. Who do you know that might benefit from it?*

You will be surprised at how many of your hot, warm, and even cold prospects will be more than willing to provide you with a handful of quality leads that you can contact using the referring party as a door opener!

You: *Hello Mr. Birch, Jerry Johnson from ABC Courier suggested I contact you to show you how I can help you save money and be more efficient!*

Once you have established relationships with current customers, the referrals become more plentiful and even easier to get.

FOLLOW UP WITH EXISTING CUSTOMERS

In some organizations you will continue to work with your customers on a regular basis, selling repetitive products or additional products and services. In other cases, you are "finished" with the customer once the sale is made and the customer is turned over to your customer satisfaction department. Some companies prefer that you discontinue contact with that customer in favor of getting new business. I suggest you at least stay in contact with and available to your customers. One of the biggest complaints against salespeople is that they "disappear" after the sale. If there is a problem, the customer may want to call you – especially if they have called customer service and were not satisfied. It's not the problem, it's how you handle the problem that counts. You may want the opportunity to call on this customer again for a completely different product.

[**It's not the problem, it's how you handle the problem that counts.**]

CHAPTER

THE EIGHT STEPS
TO SUCCESS IN SELLING

We've covered a lot of information in this short book. I hope you are so excited that you can hardly wait to get started! If you have taken the time to set your personal goals and objectives, congratulations! In the next 90 days your life could be completely different! Before we part, I'd like to summarize some of what we have covered through what I refer to as the "Eight Steps to Success in Selling."

STEP 1. SET SPECIFIC GOALS: WHAT DO YOU WANT AND WHEN DO YOU WANT IT?

Personal Goals
Sure, we're all working to make a living and pay the bills, put some money away, and live a good lifestyle. You no doubt are aware that a goal of getting by is not enough to motivate you to take the kind of action outlined in this book. Once you've paid the bills, what then? Are you really going to have enough motivation to consistently achieve your daily PAO? You know you must set specific goals that inspire you if you expect to be part of the top 20 percent. How much money do you want to make? How did you come up with that figure? What are you going to do with the money? Buy a new car, a house? Where will it be? What color? How will it feel to be there? Can you visualize yourself driving in your new car, or hanging pictures in your new house? Your vision must be strong enough to inspire and motivate you to do what you need to do, when you need to do it, whether you feel like it or not!

Write down your goals. It is proven that the 4 percent who write down their goals accomplish far more than all the others combined.

Review your goals daily. Once you have set your goals and have written them down, keep them with you. Look at them as often as possible to constantly remind you why you are willing to work harder than those around you!

[**The 4 percent who write down their goals accomplish far more than all the others combined.**]

Step 2. Make the Commitment

It's one thing to want something or to want to do something, but it's another to commit yourself to getting it. To get what you want, you have to make a decision that you ABSOLUTELY WILL ACHIEVE YOUR GOALS — NO MATTER WHAT OBSTACLES GET IN YOUR WAY!

It's not easy to make this commitment. Why? Because once you do, you have put your integrity on the line. You know you must do what you set out to do or you will have to live with yourself knowing you gave up, quit.

Once the decision is made and you have made the commitment, it's like taking a huge weight off of your shoulders.

Your goals are worth the effort. You deserve the lifestyle that will be the reward for the next 90 days of intense effort. Come on! Make the commitment and get started today!

Step 3. Develop Your Action Plan

When you've made the commitment to succeed, you'll have many battles left to fight, but you know you can win the war! It's time to set up your action plan. Take the time to learn your compensation plan and fully understand what you will have to accomplish to attain your goals. Determine your PSO along with your monthly, weekly, and daily PAO. It is a wonderful thing to know exactly where you are going and just exactly how you will get there! Pareto figured out the formula — all you have to do is plug in the numbers!

Lifestyle Objectives = Income Objectives =
Sales Objectives = Deals Objectives = PAO

Your PAO is your number-one focus. It is your first priority!
Don't set this book down until your monthly, weekly, and daily
PAO have been set!

STEP 4. TAKE ACTION – NOW!

Get started! You know what you want, you're committed to your
goals, you've set up your action plan — now do it! Jump in with
both feet! Don't procrastinate! Start TODAY!

Block out the time you need each day to achieve your PAO. For
a few good reasons, mornings are usually the best time to complete
prospecting calls. First, the decision maker is more likely to be
in. Second, you are more likely to achieve your PAO if you make
prospecting your first priority of the day. If you fall short one day,
you can make up for it on another day that week.

Although you know exactly what to expect, it will be natural to
fear what you have not yet done. So what? There is only one cure
for fear — ACTION! Feel the fear and do it anyway! After just a
few days you'll wonder what you were so worried about in the first
place!

STEP 5. KEEP DEVELOPING

We have talked about statistics, formulas, personal and activity
goals, and action plans. All of these are mechanical. You can master
the mechanics, but if you don't have a positive attitude and genuine
enthusiasm, people will not respond to you. It should be apparent
that you are enjoying what you do, are serious, and are confident.

Personal Development

You should naturally project a "message" to your prospects that
says, "I would love to have your business. I am looking for a group
of customers to work with. I will succeed whether or not we do
business together, but if we do, it will truly be a win-win situation."
Your prospect will respect you for your attitude. On the other hand,
if you project an "I need your business" attitude, your prospect will
sense it and be turned off.

To develop a positive, enthusiastic attitude:

- Read at least ten pages per day from a positive source
- Listen to motivational and personal development tapes
- Attend seminars
- Network with like-minded people

Readers are leaders and leaders are readers. If you want to build and maintain a positive attitude, find out how others did it! This is your "fuel." As you go out and exert energy day after day, you burn positive fuel. You'll subject yourself to rejection, other people's attitudes, the news (which is usually negative), and so on. If you don't choose to fill your mental fuel tank yourself, you choose by default to let others fill your tank with whatever negative garbage they want! Read, listen to positive motivational tapes, and attend personal development seminars. Fill your mental fuel tank with high-octane, positive fuel.

In addition, network with other successful, motivated people. Some people are negative, some are positive. Positive people say, "It will be difficult, but it can be done." Negative people say, "It could be done, but it's too difficult." You will become like the people you associate with. Make sure you spend time with positive people who want you to succeed!

Professional Development

I believe that anyone with a positive, enthusiastic attitude — regardless of previous sales experience or skill level — who applies the principles and formulas outlined in this book will get from zero to hero in the next 90 days. However, you can and should continually build your sales skills by tapping into the vast supply of knowledge made available by those who succeeded before you. Once again, read ten pages a day from the masters, attend their seminars, and listen to their tapes!

In addition, seek out the top 20 percent of the salespeople in your organization and ask them for advice, tips, and tricks. They are usually willing to assist a sincere, new recruit.

You can visit *www.donmastrangelo.com* anytime for the most up-to-date personal and professional development resources.

Step 6. Control What You Can, Forget What You Can't

What can you control? You can set your goals, take action to achieve them, develop a positive attitude. You can control how many prospecting calls you complete each day, week, and month. You can even control the relationship selling process when interacting with decision makers during your appointments. You can build your selling skills. Bottom line, you can control what *you* do, your own attitude, and your actions!

What can't you control? Other people and how they react toward you. The economy and world events. You can't make people buy from you. That's not your job. Look for the prospects that need you and forget about the rest for now. As long as you keep holding up your part of the bargain — your action plan — you will create enough business to keep you busy and make a lot of money. Enjoy the process of meeting new people and learning new things about your prospects without placing pressure on yourself to make them buy!

Step 7. Be Accountable, Persistent, and Consistent

Congratulations — you're off and running!

Be prepared — obstacles *will* get in your way. Unscheduled meetings, family in town — all kinds of fires will start burning just begging for you to put them out!

Don't let yourself get distracted. Track your activity every day — several times each day in fact — and be accountable to yourself! If you let your PAO slide just a couple of times, it will get easier and easier to drop the ball. Be persistent. Be consistent. Don't get in the habit of completing several prospecting calls one day and then few or none the next. We are creatures of habit; you will need to immediately get in the habit of completing a consistent number of prospecting calls daily — your daily PAO.

I have seen hundreds of individuals rise to the top as a direct result of simply achieving their PAO consistently for 90 days. However, I've seen many more fail simply because they didn't!

Step 8. Never Quit

There is only one way to fail and that is to quit. When things aren't going your way, don't get discouraged. Don't give up! Success comes at a price.

You can pay the price for success in 90 days by doing more than others are willing to do and by going beyond your comfort zone so you can grow and learn. You will be rewarded with a significant income that will allow you to enjoy the achievement of your lifestyle objectives! You will also enjoy recognition and respect from your peers and your company.

> **There is only one way to fail and that is to quit.**

Or you can pay the price for failure — it's your choice. You can't fail if you don't quit trying. Finally, you can always start over! We're all human. If you find yourself 90 days down the road frustrated and disappointed in what you have accomplished, just start over! Reset your personal and lifestyle goals. Establish your income and sales objectives. Set your PAO and GO FOR IT!

The RSS System Goal-Setting Worksheet

A simple way to set up your goals and action plan is to use the RSS System Goal-Setting Worksheet. Once you've completed it, keep it with you always! Examples are shown below in Figure 7 and Figure 8:

Figure 5. Page 1 of the RSS System Goal-Setting Worksheet

Ready, Set, Sell

The 8 Step Action Plan for SUCCESS!

Use this worksheet to solidify your sales plan. Keep one copy and refer to it daily.
Give a copy to someone not affiliated with your business to keep you accountable.

STEP 1

Set Specific Objectives: What do you want and when do you want it?

INITIALS

A. List below what you want most from your job/business:

10 things I want most	When I want it	What will it cost/ Action required
Toyota Prius	3 mo. from now	$300/mo
own my own home	1 yr. from now	$800/mo
to be in shape	6 mo from now	workout 3x wk - club dues
spend time w/ mom & dad	regularly by 90 days	build territory/get flexible
get out of debt	1 yr from now	$5000/ $400/mo
put $200/mo in savings	Now	xtra $200/mo
spend 1 wk in Bahamas	end of this year	$5000/$400/mo
ski at least 4 times/yr	next season	$1000 + time
more time w/ family	Now	get/stay organized
meet quota monthly	every month	stay on my plan

Personal Income Objective (PIO)
Review the "lifestyle" that you have determined you want to live and establish what monthly income will be necessary to achieve it: $ _2,500/mo_

B. Personal Sales Objective (PSO)
I must generate $ _16,750.00_ in revenue monthly at _15_ % commission to generate $ _2,500.00_ personal monthly income.
-or-
I must sell _25_ units per month at $ _100_ commission per unit to generate $ _2,500_ personal monthly income.

C. Personal Monthly Deals Objective (PMDO)
At an average of $ _670_ per account, I must secure _25_ accounts to reach my PMDO.
-or-
At an average of _1_ unit(s) per deal, I must close _25_ deals per month to reach my PMDO.

Figure 6. Page 2 of the RSS System Goal-Setting Worksheet

INITIALS _(Q)_

E. Review Your Goals Often:
I will review my goals daily.

STEP 2: Make a Quality Decision that You Will Achieve Your Objectives No Matter What Obstacles Get in Your Way

INITIALS _(Q)_

I have made the decision to succeed! I know that obstacles will get in my way and that I will be distracted, but I have placed the highest priority on my success. I will stick to my action plan.

STEP 3: Develop an Action Plan

A. Set monthly, weekly, and daily Personal Activity Objectives (PAO)

INITIALS _(Q)_

I know that to achieve my objectives I must commit myself to completing prospecting calls. I will complete _20_ prospecting calls per day, resulting in _100_ prospecting calls per week, and _400_ per month. If I fall short any day, I will make up the calls within that same week.

STEP 4: Take Action!

INITIALS _(Q)_

I will start my action plan as of _3_ / _6_ / _06_ .

STEP 5: Develop a Positive, Enthusiastic Attitude

INITIALS _(Q)_

I will expose myself to positive books, tapes, seminars, and people. I will read at least 15-30 minutes a day.

STEP 6: Focus on What You Can Control. Forget What You Can't

INITIALS _(Q)_

I will stay focused on my action plan. I will complete the calls and read the books. I will analyze the results of my activity for 90 days, at which time I will review these results and set new goals for the next 90 days. Review date: _6_ / _1_ / _06_

STEP 7: Be Accountable, Persistent, and Consistent

INITIALS _(Q)_

I will give a copy of this worksheet to someone I trust who is not affiliated with my business and ask them to hold me accountable for these activities. The person I will contact is ___Joe Smith___ .

STEP 8: Never Quit!

INITIALS _(Q)_

I understand that the activities that I have outlined on this worksheet are my custom-tailored plan for success. I know that when I review this worksheet 90 days from now I will be excited about the results. I also understand that the only person who can keep me from achieving success is myself. I am committed to this action plan and I WILL NOT QUIT!

This form is available on our website at www.donmastrangelo.com.

CHAPTER 11

TRACKING YOUR SALES ACTIVITY

You are now fully aware how powerful the Ready, Set, SELL! System can be for you. To follow the process to success, it is absolutely essential that you have an effective system to track and organize your sales activity. Once you have set your monthly, weekly, and daily PAO, you must be able to gauge your actual progress versus your goals. In addition, once you have identified warm and hot prospects you will need a tickler file system that allows you to schedule follow-up activities and ensure that as your momentum builds you do not lose track of your opportunities.

There are basically two forms of tracking systems available — manual and electronic. The manual system is a combination of customized forms and processes organized in a sales binder. This tried-and-true system is in wide use today and may be the perfect fit for you.

The electronic options include stand-alone or network-able versions of customer relationship management (CRM) software programs. There are now some truly amazing and powerful Internet-based CRM programs available. Most recently I have had the opportunity to fully develop the Ready, Set, SELL! methodology into a specialized software program called RSS Software. Whether you use it as a stand-alone system or in conjunction with ACT™, Outlook™, Salesforce.com™, Goldmine™, or other popular CRM systems, RSS Software is the easiest, most powerful, and most complete method to track RSS sales activity for any organization — from one to many thousands of users.

What follows is a general overview of both the Ready, Set, SELL! Organizer (manual version) and the Ready, Set, SELL! Software (electronic version). For a more in depth overview on both the manual and available electronic CRM systems, visit *www.donmastrangelo.com*.

GETTING TO KNOW YOUR READY, SET, SELL! ORGANIZER

Your Ready, Set, SELL! System Organizer includes the following components:

- Instructions/Game Plan tab
- A Pinpoint Prospect List tab
- Address/Phone tab
- A Forms tab
- 12 "Month at a Glance" tabs
- A tickler file tab
- A-Z tabs for Account Record Forms 1-4 Misc. or Projects tabs
- A Plastic Dayfinder
- A supply of two-page daily pages and all other necessary forms
- A mechanical pencil

Instructions/Game Plan Tab
This section includes these instructions for use of the *Ready, Set, SELL!* Organizer along with your customized Game Plan form.

Pinpoint Prospect List Tab
This is where your Pinpoint Prospect List resides. If you do not have a prospect list, we can direct you to a reputable source for a list of your "ultimate" prospects from your market area. Visit *www.donmastrangelo.com* for more information.

Address/Phone Tab

Use this section to record phone numbers and addresses of vendors, associates, friends, family, etc. Don't record customer and prospect information here — use the Account Record forms in the tickler file section.

Tickler File Tab

Behind this tab is your A-Z file, which will house your Account Record forms for warm and hot prospects, as well as current customers.

Forms Tab

Extra forms, note pages, etc. are stored here.

Month Tabs

Tabs and a calendar for each month are provided. Your daily pages are placed behind these tabs.

1 Through 4 Tabs

Use these tabs for special projects (personal and business). You will refer to these tabs in your monthly and weekly planning process.

THE MONTHLY PLANNING PROCESS

Monthly Goals and Planning

Use this form to record the ten things (business and personal) that you feel are the most important to accomplish this month and record your personal objectives for the new month.

Ready, Set, Sell

Monthly Goals and Planning Worksheet

Month: _January_

Commit to writing the ten most important things you intend to accomplish this month:

workout 3 times/wk   listen to tapes everyday

read 10 pages/day   reach my account goal

reach my revenue goal   stay positive

Set your activity goals:

Prospecting Calls _400_

Revenue _$10,000_

Accounts _22_

Proposals / Estimates _80_

Add to Tickler _80_

Appointments   40

Write down any other personal or business goals and objectives for this month:

I will consistently complete at least 20 prospecting calls per day!

Copyright 2005 Don Mastrangelo

Let's assume you're starting a new month. During previous months you would have made notes of appointments and commitments that will take place this next month. These are written on the current month's "Monthly Quick View" page. Insert the appropriate number of daily pages behind the next three month's tabs. Go through the pages and date each one. It is not necessary to keep more than three months of daily pages in your planner at any given time. Keep the previous month, current month, and next month's pages only. The expired months can be kept in a storage binder for reference.

Referring to the notes on the Monthly Quick View page, transfer the information to the appropriate Daily Page.

1 Through 4 Tabs

Refer to your special projects tabs. What do you need to accomplish in these areas? Plan ahead. Write down tasks under the appropriate dates.

THE WEEKLY PLANNING PROCESS

Each week, preferably on Sunday night or early Monday morning, take 10 -15 minutes to look over your week and plan ahead. Verify that all items on the current Monthly Quick View page have been transferred to the daily pages. Refer again to your 1 through 4 tabs for any tasks relating to special projects that need to be completed this week, and write them down.

THE DAILY PAGES

Open your planner to the first day of the month. Notice that it is broken down in to four sections:

- Appointments
- Notes/ To Do List
- Tracking
- Today's Contacts

Using the "Appointments" Section
Use this section to list out of the office appointments, pick ups or deliveries, presentations, phone appointments, and tickler calls that require a specific time. You can also use it to keep track of personal appointments.

Note: Always confirm appointments in the morning.

Using the "Notes/To Do List" Section
Use the to-do list to organize tasks not covered in the other sections. When planning your month you will have transferred some items from the Monthly QuickView page and from your 1-4 special projects tabs.

Also, as tasks come to mind, write them in this section.

After writing in all tasks for the day, give them a priority under the heading "ABC":

A = Must be completed today
B = Should be completed today
C = Not critical to be completed today

As each task is completed, place a check mark in the far left column.

If you did not complete the task, transfer it to the next day's list.

You can also use this section to jot down any notes or ideas that do not fit anywhere else in the organizer.

Using the "Tracking" Section
This section helps you to stay accountable. At the end of each day when planning for the next day's activity, take a minute to write in your daily and monthly Personal Activity Objectives for each area. For example, if your daily PAO for completed prospecting calls is 20, and you fell short by 2 today, tomorrow's goal will be 22.

Your PAO for each day's activity should be based on your monthly and weekly PAOs. Figure your actual performance versus your goal and the percentage achieved and record it in the appropriate area.

Your Month to Date Actual is a running total, and the percentage achieved will give you a clear picture of what you must do during the remainder of the month to reach your goals.

Appointments

7	
8	00 Sales meeting
9	
10	ABC Co. appointment
11	
12	00 lunch TGI Fridays w/ John
1	
2	
3	00 hair appointment
4	
5	
6	
7	

To Do List / Notes

✔	ABC	
	A	weekly report
		hair appointment 3:00
	A	plan next week
✔	B	Johnson proposal
	A	Read!
✔	B	send thank you note to Mary
	B	plan month of Feb.
	C	Deposit

Tracking

Item	Today's Goal	Today's Actual	% Achieved	Month Goal	MTD Actual	% Achieved
Prospecting	18	20	111%	400	400	100%
Revenue	454	475	105%	$10,000	$10,427	104%
Estimates	4	2	50%	80	77	96%
Appointments	2	2	100%	40	36	90%

Using the "Today's Contacts" Section

As you finish each of your prospecting call attempts, write the name of the account and any note or comment you may have in this section, and mark "P" in the type of call section.

If you completed the prospecting call (talked to the decision maker and determined if the prospect is cold, warm, or hot), mark the appropriate box (CWH) with a check mark under the "Outcome" section. Also place a check mark in the far left column of the page on this row signifying that you have completed the call.

If you were not able to talk to the decision maker and therefore did not complete the prospecting call, leave the "Outcome" section blank for this prospect until you have reached him or her by phone or have attempted to do so three times with no positive result (Three strikes and they are out.) Mark each attempt with a check mark in the space provided. After the third attempt consider the prospect is "cold" and mark that box.

If you want to add the prospect to your mailing list, check the "List" box.

If the prospect qualifies for your tickler file, mark the "Tickler" box.

If you were able to arrange a proposal, appointment, or estimate (as applicable) with a warm or hot prospect, mark the "Proposal" box.

If the call resulted in a sale, mark the "Order" box.

Tickler calls are contacts with prospects and current customers that you had previously determined needed to be contacted on this day. Write the name of the account, phone number if applicable, and any comment you may need to refer to in this section. Place a check mark in the "T" box in the "Type of Call" section. When you complete a tickler call, place a check mark in the "✓" column signifying completion of the call. Determine when the best time (a week, a month, for example) to make your next call would be, then turn ahead in your planner and write the account's name in the appropriate day's "Today's Contacts" section or "Month at a Glance" page if the date is beyond your daily pages stocked in your organizer. Again, mark the "T" box for the newly scheduled call.

Ready, Set, Sell

Today's Contacts!

Jan 31

M T W T F

#	✓	Account/Comment	Attempt 1	2	3	P	T	O	C	W	H	Lst	Tickler	Proposal	Order	Offer
1	✓	Tucson Exterminating				✓			✓							
2	✓	Inglis Flowers				✓			✓			✓				
3	✓	Mary's Temp					✓									
4	✓	Title Guarantee				✓			✓			✓				
5	✓	ABC Company					✓									
6	✓	Pizza Hut				✓			✓			✓				
7	✓	Smith Design				✓			✓							
8	✓	Comet				✓			✓			✓				
9	✓	Johnson Systems					✓								✓	
10	✓	Solarium				✓				✓		✓	✓			
11	✓	Carpet Collage				✓			✓							
12	✓	Aastro transmission				✓			✓			✓				
13	✓	Gadabout				✓			✓							
14	✓	Cafe Melange				✓			✓			✓				
15	✓	Elliot's				✓			✓			✓				
16	✓	Gabe's furniture				✓			✓							
17	✓	Minit Lube					✓								✓	
18	✓	Ramada Inn				✓			✓			✓				
19	✓	Arizona Shuttle				✓			✓			✓				
20	✓	Royal Pet				✓			✓			✓				
21	✓	Prudential				✓				✓		✓	✓			
22	✓	TransPacific				✓			✓							
23	✓	Travel One				✓			✓							
24	✓	Office City				✓					✓	✓	✓		✓	
25																
26																
27																
28																
29																
30																
31																
32																
33																
34																

			P	T	O	C	W	H	Lst	Tickler	Proposal	Order	Offer
Totals	24		20	4	–	17	2	1	13	3	2	1	–
%	–		80	20	–	80	15	5	20	20	15	5	–
WTD	120		100	20	–	80	15	5	20	20	15	5	–
MTD	460		400	60	–	320	60	20	80	80	60	20	–

The Account Record Form

This form is designed to quickly capture information pertaining to any of the prospects that you add to your tickler file for further follow-up. The best practice is to do the updates as you work with your clients, rather than waiting until later to record what you accomplished.

The Account Record form is almost self-explanatory, but some basic information will be helpful:

1. Fill out all the information you can about the customer, or staple a business card to the form.

2. List the target products that your company offers on the form. As you discuss them and acquire that business, indicate your progress with each product.

3. Understand the notation marks for the target products. A "slash" mark means you have discussed this product or service with the customer and you should continue to pursue discussions about it. An "X" means you have acquired an order for the product. An "N/ A" means the customer does not use the product.

4. "Correspondence 1" through "Correspondence 5" are short notations for the standard letters, Thank you cards, etc. you would send out in the course of servicing and developing this customer. These boxes have nothing to do with sequence, these numbers are simply a code for a type of letter. As you issue a particular item, write the date in the box.

5. "Novelty 1" through "Novelty 5" are promotional items you may use. Create and inventory promo items for your company. These can be anything as ordinary as a personalized memo pad to roses, coffee cups, key chains, pens or pencils, or promotional flyers for specific product. When you use the novelty, note the date in the box.

6. Take short notes in the Account History section after each contact with your prospect, and note the date. Write just enough to "trigger" your memory. Note discussions, likely dates for projects to come to fruition, sales made to them and the dollar amount, etc. Next time you call on this prospect or customer you will be reminded of your history up to that point.

Account Record

Account Name __Office City__

Address __831 N. Stone__

City __Anytown__ State __AZ__ Zip __85722__

Phone (_520_) __555-1234__ Fax (_520_) __555-1235__

Contact Name __Alan Smith__ E-mail __alan@officecity.com__

Novelty 1	Novelty 2	Novelty 3	Novelty 4	Novelty 5
12/6		1/31		
Correspondence 1	Correspondence 2	Correspondence 3	Correspondence 4	Correspondence 5
12/7	12/20	1/4		

Target Products and Services

Holiday gift guide
kick off New Year
B2B inserts

Account History

Date	Activity
12/6	completed prospecting call - left note pad novelty
12/7	sent follow-up letter
12/20	sent holiday card
1/4	sent New Year program letter
1/31	had appointment - left calendar novelty
2/4	closed deal!

7. File your Account Record forms alphabetically behind the appropriate letter in your "A to Z" tabs in the tickler section. You will track the timing of your contact with each customer using your daily pages

DAY-END ACTION

When you have finished for the day there are some key tasks that you must accomplish. It is absolutely essential to finish each of these tasks before you call it a day. Total the bottom section of the "Today's Contacts" page. Be sure to calculate totals for each column, the percentage achieved, and the week to date and month to date totals.

Outcome Section

Scan the "List" column. Add any checked names to your mailing list each day. Pay special attention to spelling and titles, and make sure you have the correct contact.

Scan the "Tickler" column. Search for any warm or hot prospects. Fill out an Account Record form for each of these, send a thank you card or other correspondence if applicable, and schedule the next appointment or follow-up call on the appropriate daily sheet in your planner.

Scan the "Proposal" column for check marks. Prepare any estimates or proposals you obtained today before you leave for the day, and schedule a follow-up time. Do not let these accumulate.

Scan the "Order" column. Enter any orders before you leave for the day.

Type of Call Section

Refer to the "Tickler" column. Make sure that you called on each account, updated your Account Record form, and scheduled your next call.

Notes/To-Do List Section

Forward any tasks not completed today.

Tracking Section

Total today's activity, the percentage achieved, the month-to-date actual, and month-to-date percentage achieved, and set your goals for the following day, writing them on tomorrow's daily page.

Take a few minutes to look over the next day's pages. Make a mental note of all the tickler calls listed, appointments, tasks, etc. so that you are well prepared for the next day's activity. For tickler calls, review the Account Record form to remind yourself where you are for each opportunity and what action you have scheduled next.

Month-end Action

At the end of each month you should seriously consider your productivity for the month. Did you achieve your Personal Activity Objectives, Personal Monthly Deal Objective, and Unit or Revenue Objectives? If so, congratulations! If not, identify and acknowledge where you could have done better. Set new goals and plan well for the coming month. (Refer to "The Monthly Planning Process" on page 80).

The Electronic Version

You can use RSS Software as a stand-alone CRM solution, or you can easily integrate it with the most popular CRM systems. Once your account has been created you simply log in to view your appointments and task list. You can quickly view and manage contacts, opportunities, etc. Each user and manager can instantly run real-time pipeline and forecast reports, review and manage RSS sales activity and much more.

For the purposes of this overview, we'll stick to a simple example of how to set your Personal Objectives and track your Ready, Set, SELL! sales activity using the RSS Software "Goal Setting," "Opportunity Manager," and "Dashboard" functions.

Figure 7. Listing the "Things I Want Most" in the Goal Setting Module

Things I Want Most This Year	Monthly Cost
House Payment	1200.00
Car Payment	465.00
Credit Cards	325.00
Vacation Fund	300.00
Food & Clothing	400.00
Utilities	250.00
Entertainment	250.00
Debt Reduction	500.00

Total Monthly $3,690

As shown in Figure 7, once you have logged in to your account you will begin by accessing the Personal Goals and Objectives module and completing the goal-setting process. Start by choosing "View Details" and listing the "Things I Want Most" and the associated monthly costs as described in Chapter 4. You would continue by choosing the "Close Details" button, saving the data to the system, which will bring you back to the Goal Setting Module as shown in Figure 8:

Figure 8. The RSS Software Goal-Setting Module

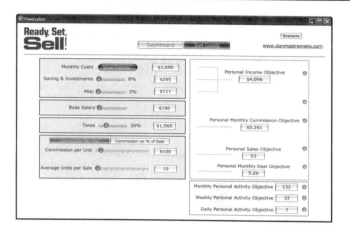

Note that the total from the above exercise is now represented in the "Monthly Costs" field. You can now set the proper percentages for "Savings and Investments," "Miscellaneous," and "Taxes." Next, choose either "Commission Per Unit" or "Commission as % of Sales," depending on the type of compensation plan you are using. Assuming you chose "Commission Per Unit," you would now enter the average commission earned per unit and the average units per sale at your organization. If you chose "Commission as % of Sales," you would enter the average commission amount and your average sale amount. If you have a base salary, enter the monthly amount. If not, enter "$0" in this field. The system will now automatically calculate and display your Personal Monthly Commission Objective (PMCO), Personal Sales Objective (PSO), Personal Monthly Deals Objective (PMDO), and most importantly, your monthly, weekly, and daily Personal Activity Objective (PAO).

Now that you have established your Personal Goals and Objectives you can access your Pinpoint Prospect List directly from the Opportunity Manager module. Typically, you will have acquired your Pinpoint Prospect List from a reputable source and it will include prospects that fit your Ultimate Customer Profile. This list is easily imported to RSS Software. When you click on any record you will find detailed information including the name of the company, decision maker, address, phone, fax, SIC code, etc. as shown in Figure 9:

Figure 9. The Opportunity Manager

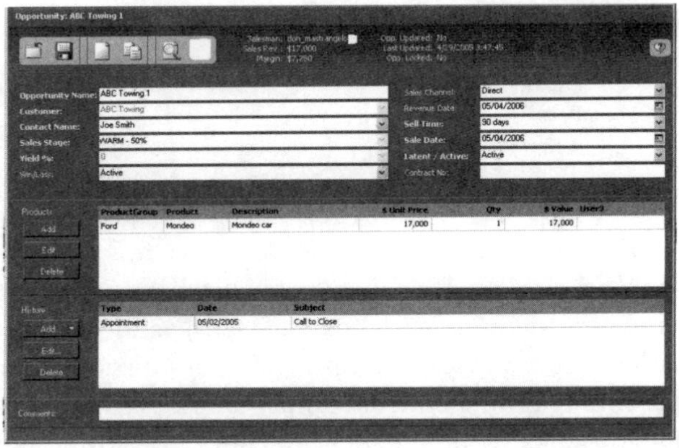

To log a prospecting call attempt or a completed prospecting call, simply click the "Add a Call" button (see figure 10), then choose either "Strike 1," "Strike 2," or "Completed Prospecting Call" under the "Type" drop-down menu. Next, choose "Cold," "Warm," or "Hot" from the "Prospecting Call Result" drop-down menu, and click the "Save" button. That's it – you have logged your completed prospecting call or attempt!

Figure 10. Logging a Prospecting Call Attempt
or Completed Prospecting Call

Once identified, your warm and hot prospects are easily converted to "Opportunities." Your opportunities make up your pipeline and forecast. You can easily run pipeline and forecast reports in real-time.

To quickly determine what you have accomplished versus your daily, weekly, or monthly PAO, simply click on the Dashboard tab (shown in Figure 11 below):

Figure 11. The RSS Software Dashboard

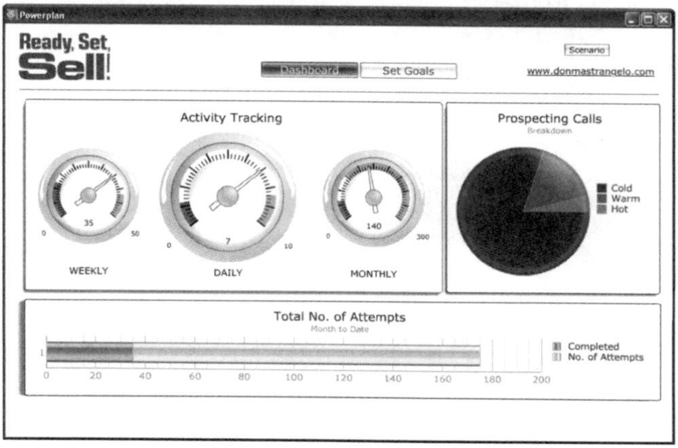

You will find a daily, weekly, and monthly "ParetoMeter" that will display what you have accomplished versus your objectives. You will also see how many prospect call attempts you made compared to actual completed prospecting calls. Finally, you will see a breakdown of what percentage of completed prospecting calls result in cold, warm, or hot. You can refresh the dashboard as often as you like, just don't quit working until your ParetoMeter is in the green!

The Manager's Dashboard reflects the completed activities of his entire team in real-time. In addition to the information displayed on the Rep's Dashboard, the manager also sees a breakdown of activity and results by each team member.

As you can see, RSS Software is a simple and effective way to plan and track your Ready, Set, SELL! activity. Once you have customized the interface to your organization, set up your Personal Goals and Objectives, and imported your Pinpoint Prospecting List, you have everything you need to succeed!

PATIENCE

Give yourself time to master the use of these systems. Like anything new it will not be easy immediately but as you start using it consistently you will be amazed and delighted with your increased activity and productivity. Resist the urge to skip any part of the process. Remember, it takes at least 21 days to develop a new habit!

APPENDIX 1

READY, SET, SELL! SUCCESS STORIES

In the following pages, I have provided several case studies and examples of the Ready, Set, SELL! System in action. These examples come from a variety of industries and individuals who have actually used this process to get from Zero to Sales Hero in 90 days! You will become familiar with each salesperson and their situation as they started to use the Ready, Set, SELL! System. Some implemented the system after being on the job for a while; others learned the system as they started a new opportunity.

When available, I have included details of the actual steps taken to identify each individual's:

- Personal Lifestyle Objectives
- Personal Income Objectives
- Personal Sales Objectives
- Personal Monthly Deals Objectives
- Monthly, Weekly, and Daily Personal Activity Objectives

Of course, there are countless other viable sales opportunities not represented here. I hope that reviewing these examples will assist you in creating and acting on your own 90-day action plan!

A WORD ABOUT COMPENSATION PLANS

As mentioned in Chapter 3, there are unlimited variations in the sales compensation plans out there. Some include base salaries, some don't. Some pay a commission on revenue sold while others pay a flat commission per "unit" sold. Some compensation plans pay upon the booking of the sale while others only pay upon collected funds. To further complicate things, many comp plans include "accelerators" that increase commissions upon achievement of certain revenue or unit plateaus. Regardless, you can find a way to calculate your Personal Activity Objectives. I would strongly suggest that whenever possible you keep it simple and build your plan around your organization's basic compensation plan features, leaving promos and accelerators as a way to earn bonus income that goes beyond your actual Personal Income Objective.

CASE STUDY #1

Salesperson: John Matthews
Industry: Wireless Communications
Position: Account Executive
Territory: Atlanta, Georgia

Situation:

John is 24 years old, single, and lives with a roommate in an apartment in an Atlanta suburb. John had worked in the restaurant industry after high school until he got a job in a retail wireless communications store for his current employer about a year ago.

When John worked in the retail store, he had noticed that the outside sales reps were making a lot more money than he was. He also observed that the outside sales reps seemed to enjoy a certain freedom in the field that he desired. John did well at retail sales and when the opportunity to move to outside sales came up he jumped at it.

John still reports to the branch manager as an outside sales representative but now he is reaching out to local businesses rather than working with customers that come in to the store. Because he was already familiar with the service plans, phones, and accessories John did not receive much incremental training. However, he did receive a list of existing business customers of the branch to "upsell" and was given instructions to call on the businesses in the area that were not yet customers and try to win their business.

Unfortunately, John had not had great success since moving to outside sales four months earlier. He had gotten to know most of his existing customers, and they liked him well enough, but working that group had not created much new or "add-on" business. Although he felt like he had made a reasonable attempt to acquire new business, that had not panned out well either. It seems that wireless phones were becoming a commodity and John was having a hard time getting decision makers to meet with him.

John knew he could be working harder but he was starting to wonder if he could really be successful at this when he learned about the Ready, Set, SELL! System. The first step he took was to commit to success. Then he set his objectives.

John decided that his main priority was to get a nice place of his own, which would cost him $850 per month. His utilities would go up as well. John also wanted to buy a new Mustang, which would carry a car payment of around $500 per month. Other than that, most everything else would stay the same — for now.

As you can see, John needed to earn just under $4000 per month net. He received a modest base salary, netting around $1500 per month. His Personal Monthly Commission Objective (PMCO) was $3127 per month. In addition to his base salary, John earned an average of $50 per subscription sold, so his Personal Sales Objective (PSO) was 63 wireless plans or subscriptions sold per month. At an average of seven units per deal, John's Personal Monthly Deals Objective (PMDO) was nine closed deals. Nine divided by .04 is 225, so John's Monthly Personal Activity Objective (PAO) was 225 completed prospecting calls to new decision makers, which breaks down to 56 per week, and 11 per day. Once again, John's most important objective was his Daily PAO, which is 11. Since John knew that he would only get through to 20 percent of the decision makers he attempted to reach, he was prepared to make 55 attempts each day, which took a few hours out of each morning.

John's plan for the next 90 days was extremely clear — he committed himself to consistently reaching at least 11 new decision makers every day and within the first few months John was able to close at least nine deals per month. This resulted in an average in excess of his original objective of 63 subscriptions and a net income of just under $4000 per month. John has his new Mustang and his own apartment!

During his first 90 days following the Ready, Set, SELL! System, John spent 80 percent of his time prospecting for new business and the remaining 20 percent on other duties. Now that he has paid the price for success and achieved this initial plateau, John

John Mathews – Atlanta, GA	
Things I Want and Need Most	**Monthly Cost**
Mortgage or Rent	$ 850
Utilities & Phone	$ 250
Food	$ 300
Clothes	$ 200
Entertainment	$ 350
Insurance	$ 175
Car(s)	$ 500
Credit Cards & Other Loans	$ 350
Vacation	$ 300
Charitable or Church	$ 50
Other	$ 0
Sub Total	**$3,325**
Savings & Investments (10%)	$ 333
Misc. (5%)	$ 166
Personal Income Objective (PIO)	**$3,824**
Monthly Base Salary (Net)	$ 1,500
Monthly Commission Objective (Net)	$ 2,324
Plus Taxes on Base & Commissions (21%)	$ 803
Personal Monthly Commission Objective (PMCO)	**$3,127**
Use This Section if Paid a Per Unit Commission	
Commission Per Unit Sold	$ 50
Personal Sales Objectve (PSO)	63
Average Units Per Sale	7
Personal Monthly Deals Objective (PMDO)	9
Monthly Personal Activity Objective (PAO)	225
Weekly Personal Activity Objective (PAO)	56
Daily Personal Activity Objective (PAO)	11

can ride the momentum indefinitely, continually investing only 20 percent of his time prospecting and enjoying the momentum of his efforts with a large pipeline, significant add-on opportunities, and a referral network of satisfied customers working for him. Then again, John might choose to expand his horizons again and re-set his objectives to a higher level!

Case Study #2

Salesperson: Gerry Casper
Industry: Satellite Television
Position: Sales Executive
Territory: Las Vegas, Nevada

Situation:

Gerry had worked in the restaurant industry for years and decided to enter the sales profession. An acquaintance introduced him to the potential of selling satellite TV systems as an alternative to cable television in the booming Las Vegas market. Gerry was working for Cable Alternatives — a satellite TV reseller. Gerry's manager, Lynn Carpenter, is the entrepreneur that owns Cable Alternatives. She hired Gerry not because of his sales experience, but because of his attitude, enthusiasm, and apparent willingness to do whatever it takes to be successful. Lynn gave Gerry a copy of *Ready, Set SELL!* and assisted him in setting up his objectives and action plan.

Because Lynn's business model includes a small draw for 90 days vs. a base salary, Gerry and Lynn agreed that Gerry would continue to work part-time days in the restaurant and work for Lynn in the evenings and weekends (which is when his potential customers are home) until he is making enough money in his sales career to give up the restaurant job.

Gerry earned a modest living in the restaurant business and at this point in time his main objective was to replace his then current earnings of just over $2000 per month with at least the same in his new venture. To earn at least $2000 per month, Gerry must sell 12 satellite systems (PSO). His PMDO was also 12, as each sale is for one unit only and Gerry earns an average of $125 per unit sold. Therefore Gerry's Personal Activity Objective was 308 per month, 77 per week, and 15 per day, assuming he worked five days per week. At first this seemed like a high number, especially considering that Gerry could expect that he would have to knock on at least 75 doors per day to actually connect with 15 decision makers. But going door-to-door is relatively fast, especially when many are not home and it turns out that Gerry could get the job done in only a few hours per evening.

Gerry Casper –Las Vegas, NV	
Things I Want and Need Most	**Monthly Cost**
Mortgage or Rent	$ 500
Utilities & Phone	$ 125
Food	$ 250
Clothes	$ 50
Entertainment	$ 200
Insurance	$ 125
Car(s)	$ 250
Credit Cards & Other Loans	$ 250
Vacation	$ 0
Charitable or Church	$ 75
Other	$ 0
Sub Total	**$1,825**
Savings & Investments (10%)	$ 183
Misc. (5%)	$ 91
Personal Income Objective (PIO)	**$2,099**
Monthly Draw (First 90 Days Only)	$ 1,000
Monthly Commission Objective (Net)	$ 1,099
Plus Taxes on Base & Commissions (21%)	$ 441
Personal Monthly Commission Objective (PMCO)	**$1,539**
Use This Section if Paid a Per Unit Commission	
Commission Per Unit Sold	$ 125
Personal Sales Objectve (PSO)	12
Average Units Per Sale	1
Personal Monthly Deals Objective (PMDO)	12
Monthly Personal Activity Objective (PAO)	308
Weekly Personal Activity Objective (PAO)	77
Daily Personal Activity Objective (PAO)	15

Of the 77 or so decision makers he reached each week, an average of at least three made the purchase on the spot. Within the first few months Gerry far surpassed his restaurant earnings and was now making much more money investing only half of the time! Lynn was so impressed with Gerry's attitude and accomplishments that she made him a trainer and later a branch sales manager. You can bet that each of Gerry's new hires is managed on the Ready, Set, SELL! System!

Case Study #3

Salesperson: Beverly Sites
Industry: Printing and Duplication
Position: Small Business Specialist
Territory: Austin, Texas

Situation:

PrintMasters is a national franchise company with locations all across the United States. Carol and Ted Kimball established the Austin location over the last three years and grew the business to profitability. They decided to expand further by hiring one dedicated outside salesperson to reach out to the small business community and increase PrintMasters' market share. Carol and Ted took the advice of the franchisor and learned the Ready, Set, SELL! System before hiring their new salesperson.

Armed with this knowledge, they ran an ad looking for an individual with the right combination of attitude and enthusiasm rather than looking specifically for an experienced printing salesperson. The successful candidate would have to be positive, energetic, and genuinely enthusiastic. He or she would have to be excited about following the Ready, Set, SELL! System. In addition, this candidate would have to be in a position to work on a straight commission compensation plan. In turn, the salesperson would enjoy a certain amount of flexibility in her schedule — provided she would be accountable for her sales activity and results, especially during the first 90 days!

Enter Beverly Sites, 30 years old and a mother of two young children. Beverly left her job as an office manager seven years earlier when she and her husband had their first child. It was not easy to give up the family's second income, but the Site's felt strongly about Beverly staying home with her children — at least until they were in school.

Once her kids were well established in first and third grade, Beverly decided to go back to work to enhance the family income and to begin contributing substantially to a savings and investment plan to provide for her children's education and a retirement fund. Also, Beverly was looking forward to re-entering the business world and interacting with other professionals, which she thoroughly enjoyed. She was very good at what she did and was a hard working, driven, well-respected professional. However, Beverly was concerned about the constraints that a full-time position could have on her schedule as she would still like to have the flexibility to get her children off to school and to be at home when they returned. She had always thought that she could do well at sales, and when she discovered the ad for PrintMasters she applied for the position. Although she had no sales experience, Carol and Ted loved her personality, confidence, and professionalism.

After discussing the printing sales opportunity and the compensation plan, they gave her a copy of *Ready, Set, SELL!* and told her to take it home, read it, and let them know how she would feel about the position knowing she would be expected to follow the steps outlined in the book. They would accommodate her schedule if she would commit to getting the work done in the time she had.

That evening, Beverly read the book and got very excited. Carol and Ted were more than willing to teach her everything she needed to know about the printing industry, and now she had the ability to create a clear and concise 90-day plan that she and her prospective employer both agreed would virtually guarantee her success! All she had to do was make a commitment to follow it. The next morning, they agreed she would start on March 1.

In establishing her action plan, Carol's lifestyle objectives included setting aside a substantial amount for savings and investments. She also added a nice sum for her clothing allowance and for entertainment, and enough to buy a new car that would make her feel good and fit her new role. She decided to include a vacation fund of $400 per month so the family could enjoy a great annual vacation. Finally, she included $100 per month to donate to church and charity in addition to what her family was already contributing from her husband's income.

Beverly's PMCO was $2473 per month. Her compensation plan was very simple – Beverly would receive no base salary and a flat 20-percent commission on every order that came from any of her customers. So, Beverly's Personal Sales Objective is $12,365 per month.

Beverly Sites – Austin, TX	
Things I Want and Need Most	**Monthly Cost**
Mortgage or Rent	$ 0
Utilities & Phone	$ 0
Food	$ 0
Clothes	$ 250
Entertainment	$ 250
Insurance	$ 0
Car(s)	$ 375
Credit Cards & Other Loans	$ 0
Vacation	$ 400
Charitable or Church	$ 100
Other	$ 0
Sub Total	**$1,375**
Savings & Investments (10%)	$ 600
Misc. (5%)	$ 69
Personal Income Objective (PIO)	**$2,044**
Monthly Base Salary (Net)	$ 0
Monthly Commission Objective (Net)	$ 2,044
Plus Taxes on Base & Commissions (21%)	$ 429
Personal Monthly Commission Objective (PMCO)	**$2,473**
Use This Section if Paid Commission by % of Sales	
Commission % on Sales	20%
Personal Sales Objectve (PSO)	$12,365
Average Monthly Revenue Per Sale/Account	$ 500
Personal Monthly Deals Objective (PMDO)	25
Monthly Personal Activity Objective (PAO)	618
Weekly Personal Activity Objective (PAO)	155
Daily Personal Activity Objective (PAO)	31

Beverly consulted with Carol, Ted, and the rep from the franchisor. They determined that the average business customer spends approximately $500 per month on printing and copying, so Beverly needed to find a total of 25 customers who spend $500 per month on her services. One of the wonderful benefits of this type of position is that once you find a new customer, they continue to spend money with you every month! Once Beverly finds her 25 solid customers, she can keep them indefinitely and only replace those that fall out for whatever reason, or continue to find incremental customers to achieve a virtually unlimited income.

Note that the standard Ready, Set, SELL! formula results in a Daily PAO of 31. The formula assumes that the PSO must be re-created every month. In Beverly's case, she only needs to create a new customer once and those customers spend the same average amount every month on an ongoing basis. For Beverly's 90-day plan, she can spread the PAO over three months resulting in a Daily PAO of ten.

For the next 90 days Beverly set out to get through to ten new decision makers every day. Of course, she had to try to reach at least 50 per day to actually speak to ten decision makers. It was not easy, and at first she was a bit uncomfortable and needed to build confidence, but soon she found her rhythm and the work came easier each day. Her day would start on the phone from her home office after the kids left for school. She would make follow-up attempts on prospects she had stopped in on or made first attempts on in the previous few days, and she would also make first attempts on new prospects. When she found warm and hot prospects, she set up appointments for the early afternoon.

Beverly made a commitment to never leave her home office to go to the shop or out on appointments until she had completed at least ten prospecting calls for the day. She knew that this was her first priority and could not be compromised if she were to get from Zero to Sales Hero in 90 days!

By the end of March Beverly had identified quite a few warm and hot prospects and had gone out on several appointments. Usually Carol would join her, lending her credibility and expertise to help Beverly win the customer. Although she could only count four solid new customers who would average $500 per month in consistent sales volume, she had a growing pipeline of warm and hot prospects and lots of quotes and proposals in the works. Beverly kept up this intense level of activity through all of April and that month ended with unexpected and very pleasing result! Beverly had won more than ten new clients, and between her four clients established in March and April's new business she booked $3800 in orders. It was getting extremely difficult to continue with the prospecting activity while running so many proposals and servicing all of her new customers, but Beverly, Carol, and Ted all agreed that the priority was following the system through the entire 90 days.

Carol and Ted arranged to take as much of the servicing burden from Beverly as possible so she could stay focused on prospecting.

By the end of May, Beverly had booked just over $10,000 in sales and she felt that although she was still just short of her PSO of $12,365 she had created the pipeline and momentum to get there.

In June Beverly booked over $15,000 and she never looked back. Still, she continues to invest 20 percent of her time prospecting for new business to replace whatever losses may occur. Beverly did what only 20 percent of salespeople ever do — she invested a tremendous amount of activity into a short, 90-day period and now she can enjoy the fruits of her labor indefinitely!

CASE STUDY #4

Salesperson: Holly Ramsey
Industry: Network Marketing
Position: Distributor
Territory: San Diego, California

Situation:
Holly and her husband Ron both had full-time jobs and were raising a family of four in Southern California. Like most Americans, Holly and Ron made a good combined household income, but there always seemed to be more month than money.

About a year ago, Margaret, one of Holly's friends started a new business as a distributor for a company that manufactures nutritional supplements, a weight-loss program, and a line of skin-care products. Holly became a customer and had been enjoying the benefits of some of the nutritional and skin-care products. Holly started Ron on the weight-loss program, and Ron began looking and feeling a lot better. He then began taking some vitamins as well and felt like they really increased his energy level.

One evening, Margaret was visiting the Ramsey's when Ron asked her about her business. Margaret explained that in addition to making a modest retail income from representing the products to folks like Ron and Holly, the larger business opportunity was in helping others to become distributors as well. Many satisfied customers like Ron and Holly had become distributors because they could buy the products at wholesale for their personal use and make a nice retail profit when representing the products to others.

More exciting, however, was that when an acquaintance or customer also became a distributor, the sponsoring party earns a residual income on everything the new distributor uses or sells. In addition, when the new distributor sponsors other new distributors, and those do the same, the potential income can grow exponentially. In fact, Margaret said she knew many individuals who had been able to leave their prior jobs after creating an income as a distributor that surpassed what they were previously earning! Margaret left some literature and a videotape that explained the business opportunity in detail, and after reviewing it Ron and Holly decided to become distributors.

During the next month or so Ron and Holly attended some training seminars and met several of the most successful distributors in the company. They learned that these "upline" distributors had started out just like Ron and Holly, and that if Ron and Holly became successful the upline distributors would also make more money. Ron and Holly were very excited to realize that each distributor's success was simply a by-product of helping other distributors to become successful — what a win-win situation!

The Ramsey's learned all about the compensation plan and soon understood what they would need to accomplish to replace their current incomes with their distributorship. They would need to identify, recruit, train, and mentor at least six other distributors and help each of those distributors do the same. It sounded easy, but Margaret and the other upline distributors cautioned everyone that accomplishing this would be anything but.

"The opportunity and benefits seem obvious to each of us, but not everyone will see it that way!" one of the most successful of the upline distributors said. "You will need to expose this opportunity to dozens of people to find a single couple or individual who sees this opportunity the way you do," he said. "And, when you do sponsor a group of distributors — all of who — have the same opportunity and potential that you do – only a few will actually do what it takes to be truly successful. Don't be surprised — expect it and plan on it." Sound familiar? Pareto's Law applies to this sales situation just like any other!

At that seminar Ron and Holly picked up a copy of *Ready, Set, SELL!*, among other training tools recommended by the speaker. If Ron and Holly were going to create the kind of success they truly wanted, they needed to sponsor six distributors who would actually work the system to the same level of success that Ron and Holly aspired to. Based on Pareto's Law and the Ready, Set, SELL! System, it was clear that those six would represent only 20 percent of the distributors that Holly and Ron actually sponsored. So, they understood that they would actually have to sponsor at least 30 distributors to find the six who would actually see the process through to the end. And, to actually sponsor 30 distributors Ron and Holly accepted that those 30 would represent only 4 percent of the total number of individuals they approached with the distributor opportunity.

Holly and Ron Ramsey – San Diego, CA	
Sponsoring Objective - Number of Distributors	30
Overall Personal Activity Objective (6 Months)	750
Monthly Personal Activity Objective (PAO)	125
Weekly Personal Activity Objective (PAO)	31
Daily Personal Activity Objective (PAO)	6

That meant that they would have to approach as many as 750 prospects to find at least 30 who would commit to the program — and that at least six of those would see the program through to the higher levels of success. This seemed like a daunting task at first! However, when Ron and Holly broke it down logically it seemed doable — though still intense.

The upline distributors had suggested that to have the best chance of success a distributor would need to have momentum on their side and get the job done as quickly as possible. Ron and Holly decided to get it done in six months. It would be a tremendous effort but the rewards would easily be worth the price. Those distributors who reached the higher levels of success lived a lifestyle that most others only dream of!

Because this business was all about people, Ron and Holly decided to spread the work out over every day of the week for six months. They knew they needed to reach out to at least 750 prospects over the next 180 days, which would be 125 per month, 30 per week, and 6 per day. Ron would do three and so would Holly — it was decided! The Ramsey's quickly went through close acquaintances and family members to introduce them to their exciting opportunity. Most passed — in fact some were downright rude about it! But they did find two new distributors to work with.

Ron and Holly went to great lengths to stay connected to their upline, and they read books and attended seminars that helped keep them motivated and inspired as they went through dozens and dozens of "No's" to find a few "warms" and the occasional "Yes!" They tried to be as outgoing, positive, and friendly as possible with everyone they came in contact with and never tried to push their opportunity on someone who just didn't get it. They knew they were executing a plan that embraced Pareto's Law rather than fighting it, and they knew that as long as they held up their part of the bargain and continued to do the work they *would* succeed.

After three months the Ramsey's had sponsored well over 20 distributors — their enthusiasm and confidence was contagious! At six months they had sponsored 37 distributors — well beyond their original goal but many had already fallen out and the Ramsey's just kept the momentum going. At ten months Ron and Holly blew right through the level of success that was their original objective and they just kept at it! It was not until after their one-year anniversary as distributors that they allowed themselves to slow down, now investing most of their time helping their "downline" distributors duplicate their own success.

They were enjoying the process and relishing the results. They had spoken to hundreds upon hundreds of individuals — they actually stopped counting at some point along the way — but it worked! The Ramsey's had done what so few ever accomplish. It was not because of skill, experience, or social status. The Ramsey's were just average Americans with above-average aspirations. Their success came because they understood what the price would be for success, and they made the decision to pay that price in return for the lifestyle of their dreams!

Case Study #5

Salesperson: Kathy Merril
Industry: Publishing/Advertising
Position: Advertising Consultant
Territory: Syracuse, New York

Situation:

Kathy Merril had been a bookkeeper for ten years, helping a few different employers to organize the accounting for their small businesses. Kathy had always wanted to be in business for herself, and she had just purchased the Syracuse area franchise rights for *Welcome Home!*, a newspaper geared toward new homeowners. Kathy was excited to gain control of her financial future through this new enterprise.

Welcome Home! is a monthly newspaper that is mailed to recent new homeowners in the Syracuse area. Kathy's number-one responsibility is to sell advertising, as most of the other work, such as graphic design, editorial, printing, and mailing, is outsourced to local vendors or is supplied by the franchisor. After attending the franchise training class, Kathy was eager to get started selling.

The franchisor taught Kathy all about the *Welcome Home!* concept, what types of businesses would advertise and why, and Kathy obtained a list of all prospective advertisers in the Syracuse area that were a good fit for her publication. They also taught her how to use the Ready, Set, SELL! System to develop an action plan to build her publication as quickly as possible.

Kathy has chosen to pay herself a commission of 25 percent of sales revenue, leaving the remaining 75 percent to cover all costs and overhead of the operation. Kathy has a substantial mortgage payment, a nice car, and she liked to eat out and go out often. She also liked to travel. Kathy's PIO is $5031 per month.

Based on a 25 percent commission, her PSO is $20,125 per month. Kathy has determined from her research that the average advertiser will spend $420 per month on an annual contract. Like Beverly Sites, whose printing customers spend a consistent amount each month, Kathy's customers commit to an annual contract, and barring a few exceptions, Kathy can count on repeat monthly revenue from all of her advertisers. Her PMDO was 48, meaning

Kathy Merril – Syracuse, NY	
Things I Want and Need Most	*Monthly Cost*
Mortgage or Rent	$ 1,700
Utilities & Phone	$ 250
Food	$ 300
Clothes	$ 300
Entertainment	$ 500
Insurance	$ 175
Car(s)	$ 450
Credit Cards & Other Loans	$ 350
Vacation	$ 300
Charitable or Church	$ 50
Other	$ 0
Sub Total	**$ 4,375**
Savings & Investments (10%)	$ 438
Misc. (5%)	$ 219
Personal Income Objective (PIO)	**$ 5,031**
Commission % on Sales	25%
Personal Sales Objectve (PSO)	$20,125
Average Monthly Revenue Per Sale/Account	$ 420
Personal Monthly Deals Objective (PMDO)	48
Overall Personal Activity Objective (6 Months)	1198
Monthly Personal Activity Objective (PAO)	200
Weekly Personal Activity Objective (PAO)	50
Daily Personal Activity Objective (PAO)	10

that her overall goal was to close 48 advertisers on annual contracts to achieve her objectives. Kathy had a plan to acquire these 48 advertisers within a six-month period. She planned to have at least ten advertisers for her first publication. She would then add at least seven to ten additional advertisers with each subsequent issue.

Kathy knew she would have to contact almost 1,200 decision makers over the next six months, which equated to 200 per month, 50 per week, and ten per day. As in the other examples, on day one Kathy had to make almost 50 attempts to reach ten decision makers, but she did it, although all were cold. That week she actually got through to 56 decision makers, of which 43 were cold, 11 were warm, and two were hot. One of those bought a quarter-page ad on an annual contract, and Kathy was on her way!

Kathy's debut publication had a healthy 13 advertisers. Her second issue had 19. Her third issue had 27. By her sixth issue Kathy had 53 advertisers on annual contracts and her publication has consistently grown year after year. She has expanded her enterprise to include editions in several nearby communities. Kathy is a well-respected, successful businessperson in her community and she credits her success largely to having an excellent product and to the fact that from the very beginning she was willing to make the decision to succeed regardless of the work involved. Her success was worth the effort!

I have heard countless success stories like these from the spectrum of business-to-business and business-to-consumer opportunities, salaried and non-salaried positions, self employment, network marketing, real estate, insurance, vacuum cleaner sales, and everything in between. What separates the top 20 percent from all the rest? Simply the knowledge of Pareto's Law and the willingness to embrace it rather than fight it.

If you are just starting in a new sales position, or if you need to start over in your current opportunity, the time has come for you to begin your 90-day journey! Take some time right now and go through the process of establishing your Personal Lifestyle and Income Objectives, Personal Sales Objective, Personal Monthly Deals Objective, and — most importantly — your monthly, weekly, and daily Personal Activity Objectives! Make the decision that you absolutely will achieve your objectives no matter what obstacles get in your way. Start your 90-day journey to success!

If you have not yet secured a position in sales, you have some wonderful choices ahead of you. Now that you are armed with the Ready, Set, SELL! System, you may never look at new opportunities the same way again! You can evaluate any sales opportunity and determine exactly what you would need to do to become a sales hero in 90 days.

Develop a positive, enthusiastic attitude and go out and find the sales opportunity that is the right fit for you. Congratulations! Because you invested in this book and yourself, you are ready to succeed and you will start your career with a tremendous advantage!

APPENDIX 2

BUILDING AND MANAGING A SALES TEAM

If you are a business owner or a sales manager, I'd like to share a few thoughts with you on building and managing a sales team based on the RSS System. This is not meant to be an all-inclusive plan for sales management. Just use it as a general guideline for managing salespeople who are or will be using the RSS System. If you are self-employed, it is also useful as a guide for self-management and evaluation.

Unfortunately, many new salespeople are judged entirely by how much sales revenue they produce, rather than the activity they apply to produce the revenue. Many organizations send new recruits into the field with only basic selling skills and instructions to "make lots of cold calls." The common result is a discouraged salesperson wondering what he got himself involved in.

The RSS System is a 90-day action plan that any salesperson can follow to success. It requires the investment of a tremendous amount of activity in a short period of time. It is imperative that both the salesperson and the sales manager understand that the salesperson is acting largely on faith that if he puts out consistent effort with a positive attitude, the rewards will come. The full, tangible fruit of today's efforts may very well not materialize for as much as 30, 60, or even 90 days. Sure, there will be immediate results, but your new salesperson is building momentum and a pipeline of quality opportunities that may take a few months to really get rolling. Therefore, it would be a tragedy to judge the success of your salesperson's activity only by the amount of revenue brought in that first day, week, or month. It is much better to judge the salesperson by his attitude, enthusiasm, and activity.

As the sales manager, get to know the action plan your salesperson has developed, especially his monthly, weekly, and daily PAO. Ask the salesperson to give you a copy of his activity report regularly — I suggest daily for at least the first month. Analyze the activity and results the salesperson creates. Is he consistently achieving his PAO? If not, you should take immediate action to find out why. If achievement of the PAO is consistent and the percentage of cold, warm, and hot prospects is in line with Pareto's Law, offer praise and encouragement. If the results don't fall in line with the process, spend some time with your salesperson to determine where the problem is.

You and your new salesperson will know in a matter of weeks whether or not he is willing to pay the price for success. If so, wonderful! If not, you owe it to yourself and your employee to deal with it sooner rather than later.

Of course, Pareto's Law has an impact here, too. Your top 20 percent will bring in 80 percent of your business while the remaining 80 percent of your sales force combined will drag in only 20 percent of your overall sales.

Be prepared for this reality — and don't fight Pareto's Law! If you are building a team of six sales reps you should be prepared to go through as many as 30 team members before you find the six (20 percent) you are really looking for.

Personally, I recommend hiring attitude and enthusiasm over experience. I've found over and over again that you can teach any person who is equipped with a positive attitude and genuine enthusiasm just about anything — and they will actually go out and apply it. Contrarily, an individual with all the experience imaginable but a poor attitude will probably accomplish very little and frustrate the heck out of you along the way.

Every candidate you interview will tell you they are committed and will follow the RSS System. After you hire them, only 20 percent actually will. It's not a reflection on you or your hiring abilities — it's Pareto's Law!

As the sales manager, you have to accept that your job is not to *make* your six new salespeople successful, it is to *require* them to be. You're going to provide a great working environment, a quality product or service to sell, and all the support they could ask for. You are going to arm each of your team members with the RSS

System. You will help them set personal and lifestyle objectives, their PSOs, and their PAOs. So, if you are filling six positions, set up six desks, hire six people, and be prepared to hire 24 more in the next 12 months! That's right, Pareto's Law says that one, maybe two, of your six new team members will actually go out and do what it takes. The rest simply will not. There is nothing you can do about it, other than to accept it and plan for it rather than fight it. Put your RSS tracking system in place and let's find out who's willing to walk the walk, not just talk the talk. You'll know within a few weeks. The process is the same whether your team consists of one salesperson, six, 600, or 6,000. Pareto's Law applies regardless. People are people no matter the numbers involved.

If you are starting your team from scratch, you should start by setting your overall sales objectives for your region or company and come up with a PAO for your entire team. Determine what you think is a reasonable average PAO for an individual team member. This may help you determine how many players you need on your team. Once you have hired your initial group of team members and have helped them through the process of setting their objectives, be sure that the combined PAOs of your team members equal or surpass your team objective. In fact, you might even consider over-hiring, knowing that many of the your recruits will fall out quickly. Sounds harsh, but I'm just trying to save you time and heartache. You owe it to yourself as the team leader to set a standard of performance and activity and not settle for less than what is required for success!

Be a leader and lead by example. Chances are you have already achieved success in sales if you are starting or already managing a sales team. If that's true then you have probably been nodding your head through this entire book thinking, "Yep, that's basically what I did through trial and error — I wish I had this book when I first got started!"

> **Be a leader and lead by example.**

I hope you are willing and are in a position to get "out in the trenches" with your team. Nothing will build belief like seeing the master in action. There is no better leader than the one who leads by example! Personally, I have never asked anyone who reports to me to do something that I either have not done or would not do myself.

Be a mentor, a coach. "Okay team, you line 'em up and we'll knock 'em down together!" Works every time.

I highly recommend starting a library containing an assortment of books and tapes on personal and professional development that your team can check out, review, and return. Don't make using them mandatory. Just make the tools available and observe which members of your team *want* the information. That alone will tell you an awful lot!

But don't you dare put anything in that library that you haven't read or listened to yourself! At one of my first sales management positions, my district manager came into my office one day and dropped off several books for me to read. "Don, these books will help you to become a better sales manager," she said.

"Thanks!" I said, looking at the titles. One of them was *The One Minute Manager* by Kenneth Blanchard and Spencer Johnson.

"Oh!" I said, "I've read this — it's a great book. What did you think about the part where…" My district manager got a funny look on her face and uncomfortably told me that she had not read any of these books, but thought they would be good for me. Unbelievable. Need I say more?

Hey, if you find yourself in the position of sales manager and you don't have significant sales experience or if you have not read many books or listened to the tapes, just be honest with your team and set an example by digging into your library with them (you might start with *The One Minute Manager*). Once again, visit our website at *www.donmastrangelo.com* anytime for a list of personal and professional development resources for your team library.

APPENDIX

GLOSSARY

Buying Cycle
The constant progression of every buyer from cold to warm to hot over and over again.

Cold Call
Same as a prospecting call.

Completed Prospecting Call
A prospecting call in which the decision maker was reached for the first time and the prospect is classified as:

- *Cold:* Not interested at this time. Approximately 80 percent of completed prospecting calls are cold.

- *Warm:* Interested in learning more but an urgent need is not yet apparent. Expect 16 percent of your completed prospecting calls to be warm.

- *Hot:* The decision maker recognizes an urgent need for your product or service and is very interested in getting more information immediately. This sale should close in your current sales cycle. Expect 4 percent of your completed prospecting calls to be hot!

Decision Maker
The person with the ability to make a final decision on buying your product or service.

Dream Board
A collage of images and statements that represent your lifestyle objectives.

80/20 Rule
A common name for Pareto's Law.

Forecast
The forecast includes any hot opportunities that are likely to close during the current sales cycle.

Funnel
All prospects are "dumped" into the sales funnel. The results of the completed prospecting call will determine if the prospect is cold, warm, or hot.

Hypocrite
A sales manager who expects his sales team to do what he is unable or unwilling to do himself.

Lifestyle Goals and Objectives
Things and situations that will inspire you to do what you need to do, when you need to do it, whether you feel like it or not!

PAO: Personal Activity Objective
The number of completed prospecting calls needed to achieve your PMDO, PMCO, PSO, and PIO. You will have a monthly, weekly, and daily PAO.

PMCO: Personal Monthly Commission Objective
The remainder of your PSO after subtracting your base salary, if applicable.

PMDO: Personal Monthly Deals Objective
The number of deals you need to close each month to achieve your PSO.

PIO: Personal Income Objective
The amount of money you must earn to achieve your lifestyle goals and objectives.

PSO: Personal Sales Objective
The amount of sales (revenue, units etc.) that you must close to achieve your PIO.

Pareto's Law
The indisputable economic law created by Vilfredo Pareto that mandates 80 percent of results will come from 20 percent of efforts.

Pipeline
Warm and hot prospects remain in the pipeline until the deal is either closed or downgraded to cold. Management of prospects in the pipeline is accomplished with the tickler file.

Prospecting Call Attempt
An attempt at reaching the decision maker.

Referral
A new prospect given to you by an existing prospect or customer.

Relationship Selling
The sales process used during an appointment to ask questions, listen for a need, test the need, and close by satisfying it.

Sales Cycle
A period of time in which sales are measured. For example, a monthly direct mail publication will have a monthly sales cycle.

Stage
The current probability or likelihood of a deal closing (cold, warm, or hot).

Tickler File
A method of reminding yourself to contact prospects in your pipeline and to keep adequate notes of all sales activity related to your prospects.

Ultimate Customer Profile
A collection of attributes including as an example the size or type of business, location, annual revenue etc. that makes up your ultimate prospect. For those who sell to individuals rather than businesses attributes could include age, income level, gender etc.

Appendix 4

Index

80/20 rule, 31–35, 118. See also Pareto's Law

A
Account record form, 86–88
ACT™, 77
Action plan development, 70–71
Appointments with sales prospect, 59–62, 82
Awaken the Giant Within (Robbins), 12

B
Blanchard, Kenneth, 12, 116
Buying cycle, 33–34, 117

C
Carpenter, Lynn, 99
Casper, Gerry, 99–100
Cold calling, 23, 32–35, 117
Cold sales prospects, 34–35, 37–38, 53–54, 63–64, 117
Commission, calculating, 91
Commission-only compensation plans, 43
Commitment, making, 28, 70
Compensation plans, 43, 44, 95–96
Covey, Stephen, 12
Customer profile, 49, 119
Customer relationship management (CRM) software, 58, 77

ABOUT THE AUTHOR

Don Mastrangelo has been a highly successful sales trainer, consultant, and entrepreneur for over 20 years. He credits his Ready, Set, SELL! System for his outstanding achievements in every assignment he takes on. With a specialization in helping the new salesperson and sales manager get from *Zero to Sales Hero in 90 Days*, Don has shared the power of the Ready, Set, SELL! System with countless individuals, corporations, and organizations. A dynamic and passionate speaker, Don travels worldwide to share the Ready, Set, SELL! System through his full-day seminars and his speaking and consulting packages. He resides with his family in Prescott, Arizona.

BOOK ORDER FORM

Ready, Set, Sell!
How to Get from Zero to Sales Hero in 90 Days

Name (Please print)

Address

City   State   Zip

	Cost	Qty	Shipping	Total
Ready, Set, Sell! *How to Get from Zero to Sales Hero*	$16.95 U.S.		$4.00 for first book $1.50 for each additional book	
			Total	

Make checks payable to: Power Plan Press
Mail checks to: Power Plan Press, P.O. Box 1788, Prescott, Az. 86302
Or fax your order to: (928) 778-5968

Credit card payment:

Customer Signature

Phone Number

☐ Visa ☐ Master Card ☐ AmEx ☐ Discovery

Card Number ☐☐☐☐ ☐☐☐☐ ☐☐☐☐ ☐☐☐☐   Exp. Date ☐☐ ☐☐